The Decalogue

*A Biblical Analysis
of the
Ten Commandments*

The Decalogue

A Biblical Analysis of the Ten Commandments

Bouvert Regulas

2012

The Decalogue: A Biblical Analysis of the Ten Commandments – published by the Rev. Dr. Ashish Amos of the Indian Society for Promoting Christian Knowledge (ISPCK), Post Box 1585, 1654, Madarsa Road, Kashmere Gate, Delhi-110006.

© Author, 2012

All rights reserved. No part of this book may be reproduced or transmitted in any form or by any means, electronic, mechanical, photocopying, recording, or by any information storage and retrieval system, without the prior permission in writing from the publisher.

The views expressed in the book are those of the author and the publisher takes no responsibility for any of the statements.

ISBN : 978-81-8465-242-0

Laser typeset by **ISPCK,** Post Box 1585, 1654, Madarsa Road, Kashmere Gate, Delhi-110006.

Tel: 23866323/22,
e-mail–ashish@ispck.org.in • ella@ispck.org.in
website-www.ispck.org.in

Contents

Preface vii

PART – A
An Introduction to the Decalogue

Introduction	3
Defining *Decalogue*	5
Historical Background	8
The New Testament and the Decalogue	13

PART – B
The Decalogue

No Other Gods	20
No Idols	31
No Vain Use of God's Name	43

Keep the Sabbath Holy	52
Honour Your Father and Mother	64
No Murder	73
No Adultery	83
No Stealing	92
No False Testimony	100
No Coveting	108
Bibliography	115

Preface

Written especially for the daily reader of the Bible, this book challenges every reader to learn the Ten Commandments thoroughly and follow them meticulously. It urgently calls for being obedient to the statutes or commandments of God.

The first word in the Ten Commandments is 'I'. The living God speaks to us as a person, not as a vague spirit. The Ten Commandments do not impose a legalistic system of rules or complicated dogmas on us. Rather, God comes closer to us and speaks to us. It is the solemn responsibility of all of us to listen to Him attentively and keep His word joyfully and gladly.

This book has been divided into two parts. The first part shows how the Ten Commandments were made available and the second part gives a biblical analysis of the Ten Commandments.

I express my deep gratitude to my friends and colleagues for their encouragement and support. Most of all, I thank God for giving me the strength to write this book and to get it published. I dedicate this book to my Master.

Let me express my special thanks to those who are in ISPCK, Delhi and especially to Rev. Dr. Ashish Amos and Mrs. Ella Sonawane for getting it printed within a short period of time by way of taking the responsibility of publishing this book.

Bouvert Regulas
May 7, 2011
Andamans, India

PART – A
An Introduction to the Decalogue

Introduction

The Ten Commandments are the heart of the Book (the Bible) and the golden rule for our communion with the Lord. The 20th chapter of Exodus is, by any standard, the most historic and important chapter in the entire word of God. These words were originally uttered by God to Moses on Mt. Sinai in the hearing of all Israel and twice written by God on two stone tablets. (Exod. 31:18; 32:15, 34:1) These were later placed in the Ark of the Covenant. The Ten Commandments appear twice in the Old Testament. (Exod. 20:2–17; Deut. 5:6–21). Both are ethical in content.

The Ten Commandments do not constitute the whole of the law. They reflect spiritual and moral principles upon which the hundreds of laws in the Mosaic law code rest. There are more than 600 other laws in Israel's constitution.[1] Among the Ten Commandments, the first four stress man's relationship to God and the last six emphasise man's relationship to man. These laws reveal God's holiness and the expectant standards for His people. The Ten Commandments are far more than ten rules to live by. They reveal the structure of our moral relationship with others. They constitute the fundamental law of God's rule. Law is a body of commandments that indicate the will of God and is a system of rules and conduct for life, from birth to death.

The Ten Commandments address itself not only to individuals, but to the whole people of Israel. It teaches obedience and faithfulness to God, social responsibility, interpersonal relationship and disciplined life. It forbids undisciplined and unethical desires and actions.

Although the Ten Commandments are expressed negatively as 'You shall not', they are essentially positive.[2]

- They are positive in *intent*. They are intended to guide God's people into a rich and fulfilling way of life (Deut. 5:33).

- They are positive in *impact*. Each has positive implications for relationship with God and other human beings.

- They are positive in *applications*: All but one is restated in some form in the New Testament as a principle of Christian living.

Defining Decalogue

Decalogue is the combination of two Greek words: *deka* and *logos*. *Deka* means ten and *logos*, word. Therefore, *decalogue* here means 'the Ten Commandments.' It is the basic law of the Hebrew state.[3] They were given by God to Moses on Mt. Sinai (Exod. 20). The Commandments were inscribed on tablets of stone (Deut. 4:13) and afterwards carried in the ark of the covenant. (Deut. 10:2).

The Hebrew word for Law is *Torah* and the Greek word is *nomos*. *Torah* means instruction or advice for life generally and not a series of commandments and prohibitions. It provides guidance and instruction about man's place in this world and his duties to God and his neighbour. It is God's guide for His children.

Law is of two kinds: (1) Direct Commands; eg., "You shall......." (Exod. 20) (2) Case Law; eg., "If a man...." (Exod. 21,22 ch). The Decalogue is the direct commands. The purpose of the law is maintaining a right relationship and obedience to God. The result of disobedience to God's law is punishment and judgement. Decalogue is an order or 'statute.' The most common Hebrew word for commandment, *miswah*, is a technical religious term that defines the responsibilities of people who are in covenant relationship with the Lord. The commandments of God are a living expression of God's own nature and character.[4]

The word 'commandments' is used in the English Bible to translate a number of Hebrew or Greek words, which mean law, ordinance, statute, word, judgement, precept, saying, charge, etc. The idea of authority conveyed by these words is that God as sovereign Lord has to be honoured. The Decalogue is a series of taboos and prohibitions that are addressed directly to the individual: "You shall not."

The Ten Commandments warn the deeds that have not yet taken place. They are instructions for life and ethics rather than law. They are formulated with great conciseness and in order to embrace various areas of life, they are made into a series. The Decalogue embraces the most important theological and ethical commandments and is being ordered according to objective importance.

These commandments were to be the basis of the whole Israelite society. They were not only moral and ethical statements, but also the basis for civil law. Their motivation is strongly personal and religious. These are not merely ten suggestions; rather, they were constituted for human society to be a successful society. These fundamental principles have become foundational to the legal codes. They are categorical and unconditional. They say nothing about the particular circumstances of the action; rather, remain deliberately general. The Decalogue is the spinal chord of civilisation. If we remove those commandments, society will be led to anarchy.

Historical Background

As we are going to look into the Decalogue deeply, we must understand its historical background. The Ten Commandments were engraved by God on two stone tablets, which were later placed in the Ark of the Covenant.

God's most familiar standards, the Ten Commandments, are as relevant today as when they were delivered to Moses. After Moses led the children of Israel out of captivity, he went to the top of Mount Sinai and spoke with God. When Moses came back down the mountain, he had the Ten Commandments the Lord had revealed to him engraved on stone tablets. We follow those commandments today, thousands of years later.

Place and Date

The Ten Commandments, which were given on Mt. Sinai, summed up the responsibilities of those who submit themselves to God through the covenant of the law. They were given to Israel by God. Probably about 1450 BC.[5] On that plain with its half-million tents, 3 million Jews watch Mt. Sinai. The plain itself is some 5,000 feet above sea level. Mount Sinai rises another

2,000 feet above the plain. Try to imagine the scene. It was a stunning view, for Sinai was smoking and fiery.

The grand old statesman of God, Moses, in his 81 years of age, left the people in the wilderness and walked up to the mountain alone firmly and resolutely. The creator had engraved on stone tablets the Ten Commandments, the backbone of civilisation. Moses received them and transmitted the divine code to a waiting world.

Its Purpose

Duties toward God guarded against idolatry (Exod. 20:1-6), profanity (7v) and secularism (8-11 w). The duties toward man protected the strength of the family and included the first commandment with promise (12v). They guarded society from murder (13v), sexual immorality (14, 17), plunder (15v), slander (16v), and wrong desires spawned by greed (17v).

The Ten Commandments lead us into repentance and to the obedience of faith. The objective of the law is our fellowship with God our Father, not our destruction on the Day of Judgment. We can fulfill the purpose of the law, when we glorify the heavenly Father by our words and deeds. The Ten Commandments are a protecting wall for those set free by grace. They have become a sign of God's guidance to us.[6]

We cannot save ourselves by keeping the Ten Commandments: that is not their purpose. They cannot even describe the relationship of humanity with God, but can only assert the boundaries whose transgression breaks the relationship. They are made not to create communion with God, but to keep this communion alive.

Giving of the Ten Commandments

The journey to Mt. Sinai took about three months. Moses recorded four places where Israel stopped along the way: Marah (Exod.15:22-26), the Oasis of Elim (15:27), the wilderness of Sin (16:31) and Rephidim (17:1-3). Two important events took place at Mount Sinai. The first was the giving of the Law and the second was the building of the tabernacle. Mt. Sinai is also called Mt. Horeb or the 'Mountain of God' (3:1-6; 19:11; Deut. 4:10; 1 Kings 19:8). The area around Mt. Sinai was familiar to Moses, because he had been with his flock over there.

Four different times, Moses went up and down the mountain, communicating God's words to the people and the people's words to God. (19:3, 8, 20,24), as recorded in chapter 19. They cleansed themselves and God came down upon the mountain to give them some of their 'constitution.' The Ten Commandments were written on two stone tablets; this probably means two copies. The Ten Commandments were the terms of the covenant that God had made with His people. At Sinai, the people of Israel accepted the terms in response to all that God had done and spoken to them.[7] Two stone tablets of the Ten Commandments were later placed in the Ark of the Covenant, the most holy object in the Old Testament. It was inscribed by God's finger twice, and the one, which was engraved the second time, was kept in the Ark of the Covenant (Exod. 25:21; Deut.10:1-4).

Division of the Ten Commandments

The Ten Commandments were engraved on two stone tablets; The first four commandments on the first table and the other six on the second. The first table is devoted to the worship of God and the second to the service of man. Relationship to God is the theme of 11 out of the 17 verses, followed by the section from Exod. 20:12-17 outlining man's duties to man; man's relationship to God and to man. There is a slight difference between the record in Exod. 20:1-17 and that in Deut. 5:6-21.

The commandments are not numbered in the Old Testament text. The Jews took the preamble, "I am the Lord your God, who brought you out of Egypt" as the first commandment. And they combined 'no other gods' and 'no idols' statements as the second commandment. The Roman Catholics and the Lutherans also unite those two commandments and then divide the prohibition against coveting.[8] The Roman Catholic Church puts three commandments on the first table and seven on the second. Josephus gives the traditional five and five arrangement. To him, the first table deals with 'piety' and the second with 'probity.' The Reformed Church accepts the 'four and six' classification.[9] Most Protestants classify in the same manner. See the table of content (of this book).[10] C. E. Luthardt gives another classification.

(1) No other Gods.

(2) No image of God.

(3) No dishonouring of God's name.

(4) No desecration of God's day.

(5) No dishonouring of God's representatives.

(6) No taking away of neighbour's life.

(7)   No taking away of his wife.

(8)   No taking away of his good.

(9)   No taking away of his good name.

(10) No coveting of his good or his goods.[11]

The New Testament and the Decalogue

In the New Testament period, Decalogue had a set place in the liturgy. They speak not only to Israel, but also to all persons of every age. With the exception of the command to keep the Sabbath, each of the ten is restated in some form in the New Testament. It is remarkably comprehensive and universally valid. Therefore, Mt. Sinai is a special scene of human history and from a religious standpoint, only Mt. Calvary surpasses it. The law of God is eternally right and is given to all of His people. They are repeated in the New Testament, for they are the basic principle for humankind. Christians also see the Ten Commandments as an unchangeable basis for their faith.

Paul the apostle used the term 'law' as given by God to Israel, from Moses and ending with Jesus Christ, who came to fulfill the law. Love is the fulfillment of the law (Rom. 13:9–10). The apostle John puts it in this way: "The law was given through Moses, but grace and truth came by Jesus Christ" (John 1:17).

Jesus Christ assured His disciples that not a 'tittle' or a 'jot' of the Mosaic Law would disappear as long as heaven and earth exist, until all of the law is fulfilled (Matt. 5:18). He approved the law (Matt. 22:40), fulfilled it (Matt. 5:27-48; 22:23) and became the end of the law for righteousness to those who believe (Rom. 8:1-4; 10:4). Jesus Himself asserts that this is the greatest of all the commandments (Mark 12:29, Deut. 6:5).

Our obedience to God's commandments comes from our desire to show our love for Him, for our fellow human beings and for ourselves. While Jesus Christ was on earth, a man asked him, "Which is the great commandment in the law?" Jesus replied:

> Thou shalt love the Lord thy God with all thy heart, and with all thy soul, and with all thy mind. This is the first and great commandment. And the second is like unto it, Thou shalt love thy neighbour as thyself. On these two commandments hang all the law and the prophets (Matt. 22:36-40).[12]

Jesus Christ teaches us in these few lines that at the heart of all these "do's and don'ts" is a focus on loving God and loving the people around us. As we think about the commandments listed below, it helps to consider how each of them relates to these two foundational commandments.

Jesus taught that love for God and love for man are the two all-inclusive imperatives. Actually, love is the sole imperative as neighbour—love is derived from and sustained by our love for God.[13] Jesus Christ commanded, "A new command, I give you: love one another. As I have loved you, so you must love one another" (John 13:34). It is the commandment that defines the responsibilities of a person in covenant relationship with God.

The new commandment defines what is expected of those who relate to God through the new covenant established by Jesus Christ.

Love is the 'Golden Rule." God is love and does love. Love is the divine chord in the Bible, book by book. Jesus taught that 'love' is the greatest commandment (Mark 12:29-31; Matt 22:34-40; Rom. 13:9-10; Deut. 6:4,5; Lev. 19:18). First, 'Love the Lord your God' and second, 'love your neighbour as yourself'.' This is the sum total of the Ten Commandments.

PART – B
The Decalogue

The Ten Commandments have been God's great moral compass for believers for thousands of years. The spirit of these ten divine commands has had a significant influence on the development of the morals and ethics of the Judeo-Christian world. History, psychology and logic strongly support the view that the Ten Commandments were conceived by a divine, supreme, loving all-Mind and that they are strong proofs of God's existence. The Ten Commandments are the principles by which the nation is to live and form the basis on which Israel's other laws are built. It applied to the whole of their lives and made no distinction between moral, religious and civil laws. It is in the form of absolute demands that allow no exceptions.

The Ten Commandments had a place in the feast of Tabernacle. At the high peak of the festival, the Ten Commandments were ceremonially recited by the priest; and in this solemn act, God asserted anew His claim upon the people. The Ten Commandments are the proclamation of His total sovereignty over them. The Ten Commandments are sketched as a guideline intended for our own benefit as well as the honour of God. They also call for reflection on how parents are to be honoured and the neighbour protected. The Decalogue indicates the uniqueness of God and humanity's relationship to Him.

No Other Gods

You shall have no other gods before me (Exod. 20:3).

We must study the first commandment at considerable length, as it is the head and chief of all the commandments. We might even say that the almost countless laws and rules that follow no more than expand and unfold this one commandment in one direction or another. The first commandment enjoins a confession of our Lord's singularity and His absolute and exclusive deity. It demonstrates that God is not a class term, but a proper name. This commandment expressly teaches monotheism, at the same time, denounces polytheism. We must keep our faith in Him as He is the one and only God.[1] We owe our allegiance to God alone. Indeed, He is the only one worthy of our loyalty—He cares for us even as we worship Him.

Few people fully understand how revolutionary the introduction of this commandment truly was. Up to Moses, human beings, with the exception of the few that God had revealed Himself to, had been slaves to beliefs in terrifying beings who had to be continually appeased in manifold ways, including child sacrifice.

Defining the Term *God*

The word 'God' in English is equivalent to *El* in Hebrew and *Theos* in Greek. Elohim, Yahweh (YHWH), Adonai, etc., are the other names used in the scripture for the God of Israel. The meaning of the word 'God' depends on the attributes and qualities ascribed to God in the culture where the word is used. The meaning of God is defined by His self-revelation recorded in the scripture. God's self-revelation involves:

- His acts in history as they are recorded and interpreted in scripture.
- The qualities and attributes ascribed to Him.
- The names by which He has chosen to be known.[2]

The scripture does not make any attempt to prove the existence of God. The God of the Bible is neither an impersonal force, nor an abstract principle; but He is a living person. People find it easier to give true meaning to existence by coming to a living relationship with Him (John 17:3). God's existence can never be measured according to time, for He is without beginning and without end. (Isa. 48:12; John 5:26; Rom. 1:23; Rev. 1:8). God is eternal and He is answerable to none. Although a formal definition of the word 'God' is not contained in the Bible, His being and attributes are displayed on every page. The definition of the term 'God', which is found in the West Minister Shorter Catechism, is the best ever found in the history of Christendom:

God is a spirit, infinite, eternal and unchangeable, in His being, wisdom, power, holiness, justice, goodness, and truth.[3]

Purpose of the Commandment

The first commandment is purposed in bringing us to love God. This great privilege was worded in the most important commandment, "Love the Lord your God with all your heart and with all your soul and with all your strength" (Deut. 6:5). Those who love God cast idols out of their lives and stand firm in the new covenant. But those who insist on their pride, see themselves as demigods and turn their backs on the real God. We should either love God and live in harmony with His spirit or hate Him and live against His will. Those who love Christ receive forgiveness for all their sins and become transformed in the image of their Father. If we turn to Him and love Him, we will receive grace upon grace.[4]

The first commandment is purposed to reject the idea of polytheism, which involves belief in many gods or goddesses. God condemns polytheism with the statement, 'no other gods before me.' In the earliest history of man, the problem was not the reluctance of belief in God. Surely, they believed in more than one god.[5] They worshipped the creature—images of the corruptible man, birds, four-footed beasts and creeping things (Rom. 1:21-23). *The belief in one God slew a host of horrors: malign storm demons, evil djinns of sickness, blighters of the harvest, unholy tyrants over life and death; belief in God destroyed the fetishes, the totems, the beast-headed bullies of old times. It laid the axe to the sacred trees watered by the blood of virgins, it smashed the child-eating furnaces of Moloch, and smashed* the gem-encrusted statues of the peevish divinities half-heartedly served by Greece and Rome.

It is a very much interesting factor that there is no commandment against atheism. Such a commandment was not needed. Fools say in their hearts that there is no God. To worship God is to worship the God revealed in scripture. We shall not worship the god whom we created, rather the God who created us. If we worship another 'god', we are violating the first commandment.

Then came the knowledge of God. An almost unimaginable person—a single being, creator of heaven and earth, not to be bribed with golden images or children burned alive, loving only righteousness—a being who demanded your whole heart.

Gods and Goddesses

People in ancient times worshipped deities and idols. The religions of the ancient world were complex. There were several gods and goddesses. These deities were much like human beings. Although they possessed the virtues common to humanity, the gods were also untrustworthy, sexually immoral and often displayed the least attractive of human traits. Often gods were thought of as owners of localities where they were worshipped.

In the sea of ancient polytheistic societies, it was a totally counter trend to conceive of and assert a monotheistic religion. Culturally and psychologically, it would have been much more logical and prudent for priests obsessed with power and influence to go along with the trend of the times and the desire of the masses. History shows that ancient peoples, be they

Canaanites, Egyptians, Greeks, Babylonians or the Assyrians, felt perfectly comfortable with having many gods. Psychologically, it was much more reassuring to have several gods to turn to and get help from, as opposed to just one.

Pagan religions have several characteristics in common:[6]

- Some gods and goddesses were associated with forces of nature. The priests and priestesses of these gods often served as ritual prostitutes. A specific god or goddess was thought to control the storm, the rains, the fertility of earth, etc. Religious rites were based on the yearly cycle of nature.

- Some gods and goddesses were associated with activities that concerned human beings. There were gods and goddesses of war, of love, of hunting, of childbirth, of education, literature, etc. As the deity of a particular nation, gods were adopted and thus concerned with its politics and conquests.

- Whereas Christianity presents itself in a historical context, the cults of the pagan gods were rooted in mythological tales cast in an imaginary past.

The masses and the priestly classes' aversion to monotheism is clearly seen in Ancient Egypt where Pharaoh Akhenaton, for a brief while, tried to force monotheistic sun worship upon his people. History tells us that within a short period, he was overthrown, and all his efforts at elevating monotheism were totally erased. Therefore, the fanatical attachment that ancient people had to their many gods, trying to elevate one god to the exclusion of all the others would have been nothing short of suicidal. Priests, at the most, might have attempted to elevate their favorite god above all others, but it is inconceivable that they would have attempted to abolish the worship of all other gods or that they would have succeeded.

Throughout the ages, humans have created a multitude of gods, and they would have been perfectly happy to continue creating some more. Israel was not an exception. In fact, for hundreds of years, the chosen people consistently tried to adopt the polytheism of the surrounding nations, and 'it often claimed the mass of the people.' The true God insisted that following illusions was not for them and intervened firmly each time they went after other gods. Only the one true God could have persevered in asserting His primacy and sovereignty upon an unwilling and polytheism-bent nation. Only the one and only God could have asserted boldly and resolutely, 'I am He, I am the first, I also am the last' (Isa. 48:12). The first commandment is concerned in the first place with the powers—spirits of the dead or demons—close at hand to the power of which the men of old times attributed so many of the operations and events that influenced their daily lives.[7]

Unlike the Pagan gods, the God of Israel was neither cruel nor immoral. He insisted on faithfulness to Him alone, but He also demanded righteousness and love toward one's neighbour.

God in the Scripture

Through the history, God has revealed Himself more fully and has recorded that revelation in the Bible. (Jer. 1:1-3; 2 Peter 1:21). The Bible itself is the revelation of God. The central truth of that revelation is that there is only one God (Deut. 6:4; Isa. 44:6; Jer. 10:10; Mark 12:29; 1 Thess. 1:9; 2 Thess. 2:5). God still works according to His purposes for His own glory. He still causes to happen whatever does happen, even to the salvation of the rebellious sinners (Isa. 14:24; 37:26; Matt. 25:34; Acts 2:23; Eph. 1:5; 3:20). Our understanding of God is shaped first by seeing His acts and listening to the interpretation of each act in the Bible. We see His 'eternal power and divine nature' by what 'has been made' (Rom. 1:20). Although God can never be fully comprehended, all these sources are important for the development of an adequate concept of God.

God's historic acts could be observed in the scripture. God created heavens, earth and all living things: And He created Adam and Eve in his own image. He established a moral standard and warned Adam of the consequences of disobedience. After the fall, when sin dominated the earth, God destroyed the disobedient by flood and saved Noah with his family. God gave promises to Abraham and He gave Israel His Law that reveals His moral character. Finally, God entered the world in the person of His son Jesus who lived among us, displaying God in His words and actions. Jesus went to the cross in order that, through His death, humans might be redeemed. Then He rose again and returned to heaven with the promise He would come again to take His own with Him. Our God is Emmanuel—'God with us.'[8]

If we are to understand the meaning of the commandment, we must take seriously, in addition, 'who brought you out of the land of Egypt'. The God who speaks here is the 'God of grace.'

Gerhard Von Rad writes:

> That additional clause in the first commandment tells us that the God who speaks in this way is not just some god or other, He is the very God who has come down to free His own people. He has called them out of the house of bondage in order to lead them into that freedom... in obedience to Himself.[9]

The first commandment is the exclusive claim that it makes on behalf of one God and one only. What we call 'exclusiveness is a modern way of expressing what the Old Testament commonly calls the 'Zeal' or the 'Jealousy' of God. This is a feature of the Old Testament revelation, which had been given to His people. But today, many people reject it with indignation. Although this phrase occurred in the Old Testament, it is to be compulsorily regarded as an essential character of God Himself. In Hebrew, no distinction was made between the two terms, the 'zeal' or the 'jealousy' of God.[10] One God means that One to whom we must look as the source of every good, and whom alone we must take as our refuge in every time of trouble. This confidence in God will be broken when man keeps secret or open relations with other powers (gods and goddesses) and ascribes to them more honour or power to help than he does to the living God. God has given His people freedom. But this freedom means before all else that Israel must separate itself from the worship of every other god.

Trinity and the First Commandment

The Jews and the Muslims accuse the Christians of violating the first commandment. They say that the Christians break the first and the greatest commandment and blaspheme God by claiming that there are three gods. They severely criticise the Christians for believing in the unity of the Holy Trinity.

Christians do not believe in three separate gods, but in one God who revealed Himself as the Father, the Son and the Holy Spirit. By confessing the unity of the Trinity, we do not break the first commandment; rather, we fulfill it. We confess God the father, God the son and God the Holy Spirit as the One and only God. The precise understanding of the Holy Trinity in the Bible is that God is the inclusive unity, the everlasting oneness. We should recognise that the unity of the Holy Trinity is concealed to anyone who has not been born again by the Holy Spirit and does not try to understand this glorious truth.

The doctrine of Trinity is distinctly expressed in the words of Christ in the 'Great Commission' and in the apostolic benediction (Matt. 28:18-20; 2 Cor. 13:14). This doctrine was satisfactorily formed in the Westminster Shorter Catechism, 'There is but one only, the living and true God. There are three persons in the Godhead, the Father, the son and the Holy Ghost; and these three are one God, the same in substance, equal in power and glory."[11]

God's Attributes

The Bible ascribes appropriate qualities or attributes to Him. God is Spirit. He is one, yet exists in three persons as Father, son and Holy Spirit. He is creator and sustainer of the universe. He is righteous, forgiving, full of mercy and full of pity. He is loving, holy, just and good. He is angry and jealous. He is Judge and Avenger. He purposes and carries out His purposes. He is wise, immortal and eternal. The Almighty is omnipotent, omnipresent and omniscient.

God is a refuge, a help in time of trouble. He is a father to those who trust in Him. God is one who hears and answers prayer. He delivers and rescues. He is Lawgiver and Lifegiver. He is our Redeemer, our guide and our enabler. He is saviour, brother and friend. He is the author of time and of eternity. God is our Rock, shield, our fortress, our strong tower and our glory. Terms like these express who God is in Himself and who God is for His people. As God is infinite, He has no needs. There are no limits to God's knowledge or presence. Since God is sovereign, people must submit to him and obey him. As God is eternal, He is answerable to no one.

Conclusion

Pagan religions stand in contrast to the religion of the Bible. Scripture affirms the existence of one God who created and controls the universe. This God truly loves us so much that He gave His own son that we might know forgiveness and eternal life. He calls His worshippers to moral and spiritual lives. He is as far removed from pagan deities as light is from darkness.

The first commandment was, therefore, the grand opening to a brand new era that was to last perennially, that would bring about freedom from psychologically oppressive and socially destructive ideas that had enslaved humanity for generations. This awesome revelation is simply the conniving attempt by religious leaders to assert their brand of religion is both simplistic and illogical. *Non-idolatrous monotheism was simply too grand in scope for humans to conceive, too revolutionary for the masses to accept and too dangerous for priests to implement.* With the first commandment, the Almighty introduces Himself to all as the first step towards the healing of minds and human relations and, most of all, towards healing the breach between man and his Creator.

Notes

1. Merril C. Tenney, The Zondervan Pictorial Bible Dictionary, 1967, p.179.
2. Fleming H.Revell, The Revell Bible Dictonary, p.439.
3. *Op.cit.*, p.316.
4. Abd al-Masih, The Ten Commandments, p.46.
5. Dan Betzer, The Ten Commandments, p.8.
6. Fleming H. Revell, The Revell Bible Dictionary, p.442.
7. Gerhard Von Rad, MOSES, p.30.
8. *Op.cit.*, p.439.
9. *Op.cit.*
10. *Ibid.*, p.34.
11. Merril C.Tenney, The Zondervan Pictorial Bible Dictionary, 1967, p.871.

No Idols

You shall not make for yourself an idol in the form of anything in heaven above or on the earth beneath or in the waters below. You shall not bow down to them or worship them; for I, the Lord your God, am a jealous God, punishing the children for the sin of the fathers to the third and fourth generation of those who hate me, but showing to a thousand generations of those who love me and keep my commandments (Exod. 20:4-6).

Introduction

The second commandment forbids man from making and bowing down to images of any kind; it was directed against idolatry. Polytheism was forbidden and allegiance to the only one God (Yahweh) was emphasised in it. Yahweh alone is God. No image of any type should be an object of worship, whether used as a symbol of the true God or as the representative of some other god (Exod. 20:4-5; 34:17; Isa. 42:8).

An image dishonours God and misguides man through giving him a wrong idea of God. A man-made idea is not a true representation of God (Deut. 4:15-18; Rom. 1:21-23). The second commandment concerns the ordinances of worship or the way in which God will be worshipped.

Defining *Idol*

Over fifteen Hebrew terms are used for idols. The meanings of such terms are, 'a likeness', 'a form', 'a representation', 'an appearance' and 'a human construction.' The Greek word *eidolon* means primarily a phantom or likeness. It can be summed as follows:

(1) An idol or an image to represent a false god (Acts 7:41; 1 Cor. 12:2, Rev. 9:20).

(2) The false god worshipped in an image (Acts 15:20; Rom. 2:22; 1 Cor. 8:4,7).

'Kateidolos' is an adjective denoting 'full of idols' (Acts 17:16). The word *eidololatria* is equivalent to idolatry[1] (1 Cor. 10:14; Gal. 5:20; Col. 3:5).

1.	aven	=	*emptiness/nothingness*
2.	emah	=	*an object of horror or terror*
3.	el	=	*the name of the supreme god of Cannan; used also as a neutral expression for any divinity.*
4.	elil	=	*a thing of naught ciphe (Lev. 19:4; 1 Chron. 16:26)*
5.	Mephletseth	=	*a fright, a horror (1 Kings 15:13; 2 Chron. 15:16)*

6.	Semel	=	a likness, semblance (2 Chron. 33:7,15)
7.	atsab	=	a cause of grief (1 Sam. 31:9; 1 Chron. 10:9)
8.	etseb	=	a cause of grief (Jer. 22:28)
9.	Otseb	=	a cause of grief (Isa. 48:5)
10.	tsir	=	a form and so an idol (Isa. 45:16)

Idols, in biblical terms, were shaped in human and animal forms. A stone or tree trunk might serve as an idol. Idols were treated as gods (Isa. 44:17-20). Any object one shapes or uses as an object of worship is an idol. All rituals and practices associated with the worship of objects could be called 'idolatry.' Idolatry is not at all an evolutionary step towards monotheism, but just the opposite. Idolatry is a turning away from the worship of the one true God.[2]

The idols of ancient men were a way of putting existence in order and so of achieving sanity. By creating idols and images of the deities they could place these forces at arm's length so that they could be addressed and placated. Through this objectification, ancient man thought himself able to chart his own course upon the sea of subconscious, social and cosmic powers that surrounded them.

To ancient peoples, idols were an essential part of life, because they regarded their idols as objects through which communication with the deities could take place. Through them, they also had a way of controlling the unseen forces and, thus, felt a level of control over their lives. Ancient priests knew the power of idol worship. All great temples of the past were showcases for attractive, impressive or intimidating statues. Idols were very powerful in reinforcing the power and influence of the priestly class. The idols in the temples were a reminder for the people that the gods had representatives who were to be feared, respected and supported, if the gods were to bless and protect them. Why would priests ever think of getting rid of such a proven source of control for a cunningly contrived false god that people could not tangibly relate to?

Artisans favour idol worship because it is lucrative. Pilgrims and devout people gladly buy statues of their favourite god to bring home and be blessed by. The abundance of this trend is supported everywhere in the Middle East and elsewhere in the world by archeologists who continually unearth small idols used by people to get protection and blessings from.

Idolatry in the Old Testament

It is not surprising to read in the Book of Exodus that, while in the wilderness, the Israelites insisted that Aaron make them "visible" gods that they could relate to and be led by. The Bible tells us: "The people gathered together to Aaron and said to them, Come make us gods that shall go before us." Aaron did not hesitate and quickly made them a golden calf as a tangible representation of the God who brought them out of the land of Egypt (Gen. 32: 1, 4). This was the entrenched way of thinking of ancient peoples, and it had become the way of thinking of the Israelites as well. Imagining, therefore, that a priestly class would deprive the masses of their tangible means of communication with their various gods is ludicrous and unthinkable.

Abraham came out from a land of idol worshippers but he renounced idols when he heard the voice of the real God. However, his relatives had private household gods (Gen. 31:19). The Israelites' neighbours worshipped a variety of false gods' physical images. The people of Israel also fell into idolatry copying the gentile practices (Judg. 2:12; 10:6; 17:3-5). The Israelites copied the forms of other gods because they did not know what Yahweh looked like (Exod. 32:4; Deut. 4:12; 1 Kings 12:28; Hos. 13:2; Jer. 10:14-15).

The chief elements in the ritual of idol worship are:[3] offering burnt offerings (2 Kings 5:17), burning incense in honour of the idol (1 Kings 11:8), pouring out libations (Isa. 57:6), presenting tithes and the first fruits of the land (Hos. 2:8), kissing the idol (1 Kings 19:8), stretching out the hands to it in adoration, prostrating oneself before it and sometimes cutting oneself with knives (1 Kings 18:26-28).

Idolatry constantly tempted the people of Israel even up to the time of the Exile (Exod. 32; Josh. 24:14; 1 Kings 18; 2 Kings 21:7). The exilic experience purged the Jews of their yearning for idols. The Old Testament takes a strong stand against idolatry. Death was the penalty, for the Israelites worshiped idols (Exod. 22:20; Deut.13:2-5; 17:2-5).

The Mosaic law strictly prohibits idol worship. Important reasons with regard to it are given below:[4]

- **Idolatry distorts the concept of God.** Human attempt to represent him in any visible form will distort his essential nature because God is Spirit (Deut. 4:15,16).

- **Idolatry represents human arrogance.** Man becomes the measure and gods are created in man's image (Isa. 2:8–22). It is merely reliance on human ideas of religion.

- **Idolatry leads to immorality.** Immorality, according to Paul, is a natural consequence of idolatry (Rom. 1:18–32). In ancient times, gods and goddesses were thought to control fertility and many rites were intended to stimulate deities sexually (Hos. 9:10; Rom.1:24–27; 1 Cor. 10:6–10). The consequence is an immoral lifestyle with sinful attitudes.

- **Idolatry serves as a point of contact with the demonic.** Although idols are nothing, the sacrifices of pagans are offered to demons, not to God (1 Cor. 10:20). Any supernatural power channeled through idols is demonic in nature (Deut. 12:1–3; 18:9–14).

The New Testament on Idolatry

In the book of Acts, we see a dramatic example of the masses' fanatical attachment to idolatry, when Paul preached Christ and monotheism in Ephesus (Acts 19). Local artisans who sold great numbers of idols to visitors were incensed at the possibility that the new religious ideas would have brought about the demise of their profession. Religious leaders were, no doubt, angrier than artisans at the thought that their supremacy could have been threatened. Both the priests and the masses had no intention of allowing foreign ideas to creep in and take the idolatrous Diana worship from them (v. 28).

No Idols

The Christians who converted from heathenism in the apostolic period were warned to be on their guard against idolatry (1 Cor.5:10; Gal. 5:20). The concept of idolatry in the Old Testament has been widened to include anything that leads to the dethronement of God from the heart; for example, covetousness (Eph. 5:5; Gal. 3:5). Idolatry is the result of deliberate religious apostasy (Rom. 1:18-25). Because of God's very being (John 4:24), no visible or material representation of true deity is possible. It prevents wrong concepts of God from taking root in man's mind (Rom. 1:21-23). Our religious worship must be governed by the power of faith, not by the power of imagination.[6]

Jesus said, "You cannot serve both God and money" (Matt. 6:24). Making possessions central in life is an act of idol worship. The New Testament condemns idolatry because it distorts the truth and leads people away from God. Thus idols need not be only graven images; they may be money (Col. 3:5), sexual desires (Eph. 5:5), covetousness (Gal. 5:19,20), etc. Idolatry could be whatever served to turn our attention away from God.

A person must turn away from his idols, when he believes in the true and living God (1 Thess. 1:9). A refusal to turn from his idols shows that he has not really repented (Rev. 9:20). When man deviated to idol worship, he lost the image of God in him. It could be restored through true repentance and by way of running away from idolatry. In the last book of the Bible, the apostle John predicts a time of idolatrous apostasy in the last days when the beast and his image will be accorded divine honours (Rev. 9:20; 13:14).

Warning to Christians

The act of idol worship produces a moral laziness and a relaxing of control over lustful desires. Because idol worshippers feel that they are free to practice all kinds of sins, since a lifeless idol is unable to punish them (Rom. 1:23-32, Eph. 4:17-19). The Bible links idolatry with immorality (1 Cor. 5:11; 10:7-8; Gal. 5:19-20; Rev. 9:20,21; 21:8, 22:15). Also, idolatry is figuratively compared with covetousness (1 Cor. 5:11; Eph. 5:3,5). The coveted thing takes the place of God and so becomes an idol (Col. 3:5).

The issue regarding 'food offered to idols' was a special problem for Christians in the first century (Acts 15:29; 1 Cor. 8-10 ch). It was the decision taken by the Jerusalem council that Christians should not eat the food offered to idols. Also, we read that they should not risk damaging another believer's life. (1 Cor. 8:1-13; 10:23-24; cf. Acts 15:20,29; Rom. 14:13-23). Moreover, those who join in idol feasts are having fellowship with the idol or with the evil spirit behind the idol. (1 Cor. 10:14-22; cf. Exod. 32:4-6; Dan. 5:1,4).[7]

When we buy food at the market or eat at the house of pagan friends, we can eat it and be thankful to God for it, since it has no obvious idolatrous associations. (1 Cor. 10:25-27). But we should not eat it, if someone says that the food has been offered to idols (1 Cor. 10:28-30).

Image of God

The Old Testament states that human beings are made in the image of God. The New Testament affirms that Christ is the image of God. There are two Greek words: *eikon*, which means a perfect reflection of the prototype and its identity. The second term suggests a cast image, which is an exact representation. (Col. 1:15; Heb. 1:3). There are two Hebrew words: *Selem*, which means image, and *demut*, which means likeness.[8]

Christ is the image of the invisible God. (Col. 1:5) Jesus, who existed in the form of God, took on the form of a servant (Phil. 2). God revealed Himself through the word and the only one physical image would ever be able to capture perfectly, the essence of the true God-Jesus Christ, 'God-in-the-flesh.'

Man is different from all other animals and he alone is made in the image of God (Gen. 1:26-27). Man exists in God's image. He is God's representative on earth. Man cannot exist independently; he exists only in the image of God. But as man has sinned, the image-likeness of God is not clear in humanity today. But the image was not totally lost (James 3:9). Through God's work in our lives, 'we are being renewed in knowledge, in the image of our creator (Col. 3:10). The followers of Christ are currently being transformed into Christ-likeness (2 Cor. 3:18).

Modern-day Idols

The essence of idolatry is not, for us, a piece of wood or a piece of rock; rather, it is the consideration of God to be anything other than what He truly is. When we start to think of God as being anything other than who He really is, that is idolatry. To worship God is to worship the God revealed in scripture.

We must be careful that this is not a commandment against art or sculpture. It is a commandment against anything that might take God's rightful place in our understanding. It is a prohibition against substituting anything for the reality of God. If so, these become our graven images.[9]

God condemns polytheism—no other gods and no idols. There was no commandment against atheism, because early man believed in God. But now, atheism became an act of idolatry, because God was substituted by human wisdom. God condemns atheism. The Bible says, "The fool says in his heart, 'there is no God'" (Ps. 53:1).

A new mode of idol worship has permeated industrial countries, while man relies more on modern technology than on the living God. The car has become an idol for modern people. The Israelites danced around the golden calf; modern civilisation revolves around the latest car model. Man became a slave to modern technology. People often idolise cinema stars and sports champions as though they were gods. We should never love or trust them more than God. There is a temptation of idol worship, which manifests in people defying their rulers. According to the Bible, cursed is the man who 'trust in man' (Jer. 17:5). Moreover, loving money is an act of idolatry. Jesus said, "You cannot serve both God and money" (Matt. 6:24; 19:24. 1 Tim. 6:9). "For the love of money is the root of all kinds of evil."

Idol worship takes various forms today because of the void created by backsliding from God. We should examine ourselves from time to time and see if there are big or small idols that stand between us and the Lord. They may be books, jewellery, portraits, memories, hobbies, habits, money and so on. Sometimes people will capture our hearts from loving God first and most. Our God is jealous and he wants to possess us complete. The ancient and modern idols must disappear from our lives. We should renew our commitment to our Heavenly Father again.

Conclusion

Images are tangible and, therefore, reassuring. Worshipping a spiritual, invisible Being would have been psychologically impossible to accept by a primitive, unsophisticated, idol-worshipping society, if it was only asserted by a priestly class. The God of the Bible insisted that His people had to do the inconceivable: abandon the natural tendency to worship what can be seen and worship what cannot be seen.

What a noble idea it was to worship a Being that no sculpture or picture could ever represent. What a revolutionary concept it was to abandon the reassurance of tangible gods for One that is, yet cannot be seen. History, culture, psychological habits and needs, entrenched religious ideas and commerce, all cooperated against the rise and assertion of non-idolatrous monotheism. Yet, it emerged; yet it survived; yet it prevailed. The reason for this is simple: The invisible God is, and He prevailed over lies and deceit.

Notes

1. W. E Vine, An Expository Dictionary of The New Testament Words, pp.243-244.
2. Fleming H. Revell, The Revell Bible Dictionary, p.510.
3. Merril C. Tenney, (Gen.Ed.) The Zondervan Pictorial Bible Dictionary, p.368.

4. *Op.Cit.*, p.511.

5. *Ibid.*, p.442.

6. Mathew Henry's Commentary, p.124.

7. Merril C. Tenney (Gen. Ed) The Zondervan Pictorial Bible Encyclopaedia, p.370.

8. Fleming H. Revell, The Revell Bible Dictionary, p.512.

9. Dan Betzer, The Ten Commandments, p.13.

No Vain Use of God's Name

You shall not misuse the name of the Lord your God, for the Lord will not hold anyone guiltless who misuses his name (Exod.20:7).

Introduction

The third commandment signifies the reverence of Jehovah's name. Name and person were equivalent in the Old Testament. This commandment is the prohibition of blasphemy and profanity. It also condemns immorality and anything that causes God's honour to suffer defilement by the sinner who bears His name. It is given with respect to the sacredness and significance of God's name. The application of this commandment is that you should guard your speech and strive to communicate effectively and respectfully.

The word 'vain' is used in KJV for the word 'misuse.' It is equivalent to some Greek words:

- *Kenos* means empty
- *Mataioo* means to make vain or foolish
- *Eike* means vainly or without any purpose[1]

'Misuse' here means to treat God's name with contempt by speaking lightly of him or by acting as if he were irrelevant to daily life. It is slanderous or abusive speech directed towards God. Blasphemy against God can involve cursing or reviling God or treating him with contempt. By the word, 'misuse', it is assumed that it is prohibiting the use of God's name in magical formulas or incantations.

Names of God

Most biblical names have meaning. In Hebrew culture, a name expressed something about the essential nature or character of the thing or person named. Scripture gives many different names to God. These names reveal God's character.

El and *Elohim* are the words used in the Hebrew language for the term 'God' in English. *Theos* is the Greek word for the same. These were the generic terms used in scripture of the true God and the gods and goddesses worshipped by other people.

El

The term 'God' is equivalent to *El* (Heb), *Elah* (Aramaic), *ilah* (Arabic) and *ilu* (Akkadian). *El* is used 200 times in the Old Testament. There were three uses for this term:

1. Generic name for God in ancient Semitic languages

2. The proper name of the chief god in Canaan

3. In scripture, a designation of the one true 'God'

The word *El* is often combined with other nouns and adjectives to indicate the true God (*El-shaddai; El-olam*) in the same way that we capitalise God to distinguish the Lord from other gods.

El probably comes from the Hebrew root *wl*, which means to be strong, and *ul* is its Arabic root.²

Elohim

Elohim is the earliest name of God in the Old Testament. Jesus has quoted as using a form of name from cross ("Eli", "Eloi"; Matt. 27:46; Mark 15:34). The word *Elohim* is found over 2,500 times in the Old Testament. Although it is plural in form, it is used with singular verbs and adjectives. Some linguistic scholars opined that the plural indicates Majesty of Magnitude. It is also suggested that it implies the trinity of the Bible's 'One God'. *Elohim* remains a general name in the sense that it stands for God as creator and supreme being.³

Jehovah

The word *Jehovah* probably never existed in the Hebrew language. Originally, Hebrew was written with consonants only, the readers supplying the vowels as they read. The word from which *Jehovah* or *Jahweh* comes consists of the consonants 'YHWH' and was probably pronounced 'Yahewh'. When the Jews read scriptures, they never used the word YHWH; rather, they substituted the word 'Adonai' meaning 'Lord' or 'Master.' Jehovah was the one and only true God (Exod. 4:22; 32:27; Deut. 6:4; 1 Sam. 17:45).

Yahovah is the personal name of the God of the Old Testament. It is His covenant name by which He was made known to His people, Israel. Yahweh means, 'The One who Is Always Present." The name YHWH was connected with the Hebrew words "I am." Therefore, the term YHWH may be translated "I am who I am", or 'I will be what I will be."[4] The name Jehovah belongs especially to Him when He is dealing with its own, while God is used more when dealing with the gentiles. Yahweh is associated with his saving work and covenant relationship with His people.

Sinful Use of the Name of God

The true God uses one more opportunity to assert Himself, by stressing the need to show respect for the One who created and sustains humans. God's name represents the Almighty. Lack of respect for His name will lead to lack of respect for Him and for His ways. This commandment is meant to elicit complete and well deserved awe for the origin of life. If God exists, and if He were to manifest Himself to humans, would He not demand complete respect? He has the right to expect total reverence and submission. And so He did.

To take God's name in vain is to use His holy name unworthily or to no good purpose, which is in turn to consider 'God' an empty or meaningless word. God's revealed name is Yahweh, which means 'the One who is always present' or He who is or He who has eternal and unconditional existence. God knew that people would have used His name to support false oaths and ideas. God demanded that His name never be used to support falsehood and deceit (Lev. 19:12). The Israelite who speaks the name of the Lord must act in truth, for the Lord's name is truth. He also demanded that His name not be used to support the magical thinking of the time, when the names of gods were thought to have magical powers. Thus, the third commandment came crushing down on the heads of the black magicians. The Lord was a Lord of righteousness; He was not to be invoked for evil deeds.

The verb *nasa*, which is here translated 'take', connotes more than simply to use. It is a verb which is used to mean 'lift up your hand', 'lift up your voice', or 'lift up your prayers.'[5] It is often employed in cultic situations. To lift up the name of God might well mean to worship God in the cult. In effect, the commandment says that if you use the name of God, be sure you mean what you say. It is directed *against the priest of Yahweh* who lifts up God's name in order to further his own ambitions against the elder who parades his religion in order to win friends and influence people, against the theologian who has become so accustomed to the name of God that it rolls off his tongue without thought or reverence.

People usually misuse the name of God in the following ways:

- By hypocrisy: Making a profession of God's name, but not living up to that profession. The worship of such people is vain (Matt. 15:7,9); their oblations are vain (Isa. 1:11,13); their religion is vain (James 1:26).

- By covenant-breaking: If we make promises to God, yet not performing it to the Lord, we take his name in vain (Matt. 5:33).

- By rash swearing: Mentioning the name of God or any of his attributes, in the form of an oath, without any just occasion or due application to no good purpose.

- By false swearing (Matt. 5:33): One part of the religious regard the Jews were taught to pay to their God was to swear by His name. (Deut. 10:20).

- By using the name of God lightly or carelessly and without any regard to its awful significance.[6]

Someone misuses the name of God while he or she turns into charms and spells, or into jest and sport. Woe to anyone who purposely twists the word of God, ridicules it or jokes about. They would be abusing the name that is above all names and showing no fear or respect for Him.

Blaspheming God

The Greek word 'blasphemia' means bad or insulting language directed towards God, usually referred to as a curse. According to the law of Moses, blasphemy was an act, not merely of disrespect to God, but of rebellion against God. The Israelites, by nature, had a reverence for the name of God and were not as likely to speak blasphemously of God as the gentiles were. (2 Kings 19:6-22; Ps. 74:10,18). But they often acted blasphemously (Ezek. 20:27-28).

Some people deliberately curse God and His Christ. They rebel against the father, the son and the Holy Spirit. Blaspheming God is a form of yielding to demons. Many demon-possessed people became so blind that while thinking that they were serving God, were really fighting Him and His messiah (John 15:19-21; 16:1-3). Responsible pious leaders were the ones who sentenced Jesus to death, claiming that He blasphemed God. In their zeal, they blasphemed their anointed Messiah. Muslims have inherited the Jew's aversion and harbour a relentless hatred for the crucified son of God, by which they express their blasphemy against God the Father, the Son and the Holy Spirit. In addition, some backsliding Christians push their blasphemy against God by distorting the Lord's Prayer with dirty words and meanings.[7]

The blasphemy of the Holy Spirit is a sin that Jesus said, could not be forgiven. God could forgive people's doubts and misunderstandings, but he would not forgive their deliberate rejection of God's activities. When people called God's Spirit Satan and called good evil, they put themselves in a position where there was no way of acknowledging God's goodness. There was no way of receiving his forgiveness (Matt. 12:22-32; Mark 3:28-30, Luke 12:10). A person truly contemptuous of God and His Spirit would not be concerned in the slightest about his or her relationship with God. Those who consciously reject the work of the Spirit of God cannot find forgiveness.[8] In Israel, the penalty for blasphemy of God was death by stoning (Lev. 24:10-23; Acts 6:11; 7:58).

God's Warning

The third commandment warns and preserves us from speaking the name of the Lord in vain. God's people should never be thoughtless about speaking the name of God. Innumerable Christians chant thoughtlessly their prayers like a mother who sings to her child. Theologians are sometimes on the brink of violating the third commandment and grieving the Holy Spirit when they study and discuss the attributes and miraculous works of God.

This commandment is a prohibition given to you and me by God Himself to cause us to keep on living fruitful and spiritual lives. It clearly says to us that we should not glibly claim God's name without a life that backs it up. We are not to carry the name of the Lord for nothing or should not misuse it. The Jews took seriously the third commandment, for the Lord will not hold anyone guiltless who misuses his name.[9]

People hardly trust one another these days because they do not tell the truth even when swearing in the name of the Lord. Jesus forbids us swearing, simply let your 'yes' be 'yes' and your 'no, 'no' (Matt. 5:37). The third commandment warns us against swearing. When one blasphemes or misuses God's name, he shall be put to death (Lev. 24:14–16).

Speaking the Name of God Properly

The third of the Ten Commandments does not prevent us to speak the name of God in the right spirit. It contains the great promise if you confess it in faith, love and thankfulness. We must call upon the name of the Lord; at the same time, we need to be careful enough not to misuse the name of the Lord.

If a person is distressed through thinking he cannot be forgiven because of some blasphemy he has spoken, he should realise that his distress is a sure sign that he has been forgiven. The sin Jesus condemned is a rashly spoken curse and a deliberate refusal of God; not a single act but a persistent attitude. As long as a person stubbornly persists in that attitude, he cannot be forgiven.

We should use the name of God properly so that we do not break this commandment and fall into judgment. We should deepen our knowledge of the name of Jesus and its power. He forgives us our sins completely for the sake of the atoning death of Jesus and grants us the power of His own life through the indwelling of His Holy Spirit.

Conclusion

Believing that humans concocted this commandment to control the masses is incongruous and illogical. Once again, this is also a strong proof of God's reality, His love for what is just and true and his concern that righteousness prevails among His people. The source of this commandment is not human but divine. The God who enunciated it is a God of total righteousness who demands total righteousness from all His followers, especially those who represent Him.

Notes

1. W. E. Vine, An Expository Dictionary of the New Testament, p.181.
2. Fleming H. Revell, The Revell Bible Dictionary, p.332.
3. *Ibid.*, p.339.
4. Don Fleming, Bible Knowledge Dictionary, p.468.
5. *Op. Cit.*, p.440.
6. Mathew Henry's Commentary, p.124.
7. Abd Al-Masih, The Ten Commandments, pp.78-80.
8. Fleming H. Revell, The Revill Bible Dictionary, p.332.
9. *Op. cit.*, pp.74-78.

Keep the Sabbath Holy

Remember the Sabbath day by keeping it holy. Six days you shall labour and do all your work, but the seventh day is a Sabbath to the Lord your God. On it you shall not do any work, neither you, nor your son or daughter, nor your manservant or maidservant, nor your animals, nor the alien within your gates. For in six days the Lord made the heavens and the earth, the sea and all that is in them, but he rested on the seventh day. Therefore, the Lord blessed the Sabbath day and made it holy (Exod. 20:8-11).

Introduction

From the beginning of human existence, God wanted people to find true rest through coming into a living relationship with their Creator. The one-day-in-seven rest is a remainder of them that when work so dominates them that they have no time to cease from it. Restful contemplation is as essential as energetic activity in the worship and service of God.

When God formally established Israel as His people and gave them His laws, one of the laws was that they had to rest from their work on every seventh day. The early Christians substituted Sunday, the day of Jesus' resurrection, for the Sabbath as their holy day. We can still observe the spirit of this Command as we set time aside to remember the Lord, to worship Him and to rejoice in Him.

Terminology

The Hebrew word *Sabath* means rest or cessation of activity. In Greek, *Sabbaton* means to desist, cease or rest. Its equivalent in Arab is *sabata*, which means 'to intercept', 'interrupt.'[1] *Sabbatum* is the Babylonian word. The idea from these root words is not that of relaxation or refreshment, but cessation from activity. Among the Hebrews, the Sabbath was associated with the idea of rest, worship and divine favour, not certain taboos. It was the weekly day of rest and worship for the Jews.

The Sabbath is described mainly in connection with three important aspects in the Old Testament:

1. The Seventh day of the Hebrew week, a holy day set aside to honour the Lord (Exod. 20:8-11).

2. A special festival day that shared features of the weekly Sabbath (Lev. 16:31; 23:24,32,39).

3. Every seventh year during which crops were not to be planted (Lev. 25:2-6; 26:34, 35,43), a Sabbatical year.

The Bible lays down the principle that one day in seven, the "Sabbath", is to be observed as a day holy to God. The Sabbath was a gift from God for remembrance of Him. This commandment enjoins the observance of Jehovah's day.

Origin of Sabbath

The fourth commandment is based on the fact that God Himself rested on the seventh day from His creative labour (Gen. 2:2). Therefore, the Sabbath is a creation ordinance. (Exod. 20:8-11). Although the word 'Sabbath' is not found in the account of creation, the root from which the word is derived occurs (Gen. 2:2). It should not be misunderstood that God rested on the seventh day because He is a weary worker in need of rest. Before God thundered the Sabbath commandment, humans had no God-imposed, cyclical, weekly pause that would restore them spiritually, mentally and physically. God blessed and made holy the seventh day in the creation week (Gen. 2:1-3).

Some have suggested that the 'Sabbath' is derived from a Babylonian practice. But the Babylonians had a five-day week and their Sabbaths were not the days of cessation of labour. The attempt to trace the roots of the Sabbath to Babylon's evil days and the Hebrew Sabbath is more striking than similarities.[2] No doubt there were almost universal customs of keeping days of rest, but it is difficult to know to what extent they were kept, or how they were kept. Some have speculated that the Sabbath finds its roots in the Babylonian 'Dies Nefasti' that were kept on the seventh, fourteenth, twenty-first and twenty-eighth days of some months. This hypothesis is weakened by the fact that the Babylonians had five-day week cycles and by the fact that Babylonian tablets indicate that work projects had no interruption on the seventh day.

The Sabbath was a day of rest and joy, while the Babylonian "Dies Nefasti" were days of prohibitions, especially for kings. Any supposed similarity with the Akkadian shapattu" holds little weight, as it was the fifteenth day of the month, the day of the full moon. This day is now believed to have been a propitious day in which the king sought to appease the gods, but there is no evidence that it was a day of cessation of work.

People in general recognised, even from the early period, a week of seven days and God's people in particular ceased their work one day in seven (Gen. 8:10,12; 29:27). They did it for two purposes: (1) To set a day apart for God and (2) to rest from their daily work.

Sabbath in the Old Testament

Most probably, the presence of cyclical days of rest in Middle Eastern societies may have been what had survived of the original Sabbath keeping, as commanded by God to Noah and his sons. Their descendants may have kept the Sabbath for generations until transformations in meaning and approach may have taken place.

The commandment about the Sabbath relates to the promise of Israel's residence in Canaan as does the whole law. (Deut. 5:33). Sabbath legislation was an integral part of the Old Testament law (Lev. 19:3,30). As it is a gift from God to remember Him, it had a humanitarian purpose in which slaves were shown mercy by being allowed a regular rest (Deut. 5:14f).

The law of God commanded that they should rest on every seventh day from their work. Working animals such as oxen and donkeys also had rest one day in seven. (Deut. 5:14; Neh. 13:15-21). The importance of Sabbath-keeping was demonstrated by the death sentence being pronounced on a Sabbath-breaker (Num. 15:32; Exod. 20:8-11;31:13-17; Deut. 5:15).

The prophets called for right observance of Sabbath (Isa. 56:2; 58:13; Hos. 2:11). Some were displeasing to God because they used the Sabbath for their own pleasure without concern for God. Others used it for money-making activities. (Amos. 8:5; Isa. 58:13-14; Jer. 17:21-23). The Jewish Sabbath-keeping was not pleasing to God because of the wrong attitudes of many people.

A sabbatical year was the year of rest for the land. The Jews celebrated every seventh year as the Sabbath year. All farming land was given rest from agricultural activity. No new crops were to be planted. All outstanding debts were to be cancelled (Lev. 25:1-7; Deut. 15:1-18). If anyone is disobedient, he will be driven out of the land (Lev. 26:34-43; Jer. 34:13-22, 2 Chron. 36:20-21). This principle does not lie in the soil Chemistry; rather, in the disclosure that the seventh year of rest is a Sabbath of rest both for the land and for the Lord (Lev. 25:2,4). Also, man must understand that he is not the sole owner of the soil and he does not hold property perpetually. The Israelites must know that he was a slave in Egypt (Lev. 25:23, Deut. 15:15). Generosity is motivated by gratitude.[3]

After the Exile, the emphasis was again laid upon observance of the Sabbath day. The pre-exilic ban on engaging in commercial transactions on the Sabbath or carrying burdens on that day was reinforced by Nehemiah (Amos. 8:5, Jer. 17:21; Neh. 10:31; 13:15-22). Over the next few centuries, the teachers of the law built up a system of countless Sabbath regulations to add to the simple requirements of the Law of Moses. In doing so, they disregarded the word of God (Mark 3:23-24; John 5:10; Acts 1:12; Luke 13:3-4).

Significance of the Sabbath

The Sabbath commandment had a special significance as a sign between God and Israel as a nation. For both humanitarian (Amos 8:5-6) and religious reasons, one day of rest in every seven is a blessed necessity. A Sabbath, as commemorating a finished redemption, serves man's physical and spiritual welfare simultaneously (Mark 2:27). Here we find an indication of God's concern for our total being and His desire to meet our needs.

As a holy day of rest, Sabbath is a reminder to each Israelite generation of their roots and their identity as God's covenant people. Sabbath is the commemoration of both, the seventh day of the creation week and God's deliverance of Israel from slavery in Egypt (Deut. 5:15). It also served as the symbol of God's covenant with Israel.[4] Therefore, Sabbath-keeping was a measure of Israel's commitment to its relationship with the Lord (Exod. 31:12-17; Isa. 58:13,14).

God rested on the Sabbath. So, He commanded Israel to keep Sabbath and to refrain from work. It is a sign between Yahweh and His people (Exod. 20:8; Lev. 23:3; Exod. 31:12-17).

Several aspects make the Sabbath rise high above any other human-devised days. The Sabbath was to remind Israel that

Yahweh, who created all things, and who had delivered them from Egypt, was their saviour and God, and that they had to set aside sacred time to 'reconnect' with Him weekly, so as to maintain a strong spiritual relationship. The equalising power of the Sabbath shall have to be effectively emphasised. "Although one Jew may have peddled onions and another may have owned great forests of lumber, on the Sabbath, all were equal, all were kings, all basked in the glory of the seventh day. . . On the Sabbath, there were neither banker nor clerk, neither farmer nor hired hand, neither rich nor poor. There were only the Jews hallowing the Sabbath.

The keeping of the Sabbath was to be a day that celebrated the dignity of man, the epitome of God's physical creation. Among all living beings, he was given the privilege of knowing God and of enjoying a special relationship with Him. This physical being also had the special opportunity to meet with His Creator weekly, so as to be instructed in His ways and thus deepen his knowledge of Him.

The Sabbath is a gift from God to all humans—no one excepted—to contribute to their mental, physical and social well-being. As Christ reminds us in the New Testament, "The Sabbath was made for man" (Mark 2:27). It was made to benefit humanity not to limit its potential. This is, undeniably, a manifestation of divine love.

The Sabbath was to be a day of joy, not a gloomy day of bad omen, as celebrated by the Babylonians. It was specially a day of joy for the weak and the oppressed, such as servants, slaves and animals (Exod. 20:10; Deut. 5:14). God demanded that masters allow their servants and slaves to rest as well. It is a divine command from the Highest Power of all. Can we see how benevolent and how divine that is? Forcing everyone to stop and rest; commanding families to rest together a full day a week and be recharged; stopping all trade and commerce so as to give everyone, rich and poor, master or slave, a chance to be refreshed, is both revolutionary and powerful in impact.

Jesus and the Sabbath

The rabbis regarded the Sabbath as an end in itself, but Jesus taught that the Sabbath was made for man's benefit and that man's need must take precedence over the law of the Sabbath (Matt. 12:1-14; Mark 2:23-3:6; Luke 6:1-11; John 5:1-18). He said that He is the Lord of the Sabbath and it was lawful to do good on the Sabbath (Matt. 12:12; Mark 2:28). Jesus answered their criticism by referring to the humanitarian aspect of Sabbath legislation.

Jesus went to the synagogue on the Sabbath day, as was the custom (Luke 4:16; Matt. 5:17). His observance of Sabbath was in accordance with the Old Testament prescription. But He pointed out that it was not wrong to eat on the Sabbath and to do good on that day. Healing the sick is a work of mercy because the Lord of Sabbath is merciful[5] (Luke 13:10-17; 14:1-6; John 5:1-18).

Jesus strongly condemned the Judaistic legalism on the Sabbath, identifying Himself as the Lord of the Sabbath. Life is more important than ritual. Sabbath was given to man and man is not for Sabbath. God gave Sabbath to man for his benefit, not for his discomfort. The Sabbath was intended to ease man's burden, not to harden it (Matt. 12:1-8; 23:4).

Christian Concept of Sabbath

Christians are not at all slaves to the Israelite law; therefore, we are free from the bondage of the law. But God wants His people to find true rest through coming into a living relationship with our Creator. We must also enjoy the created world and all our activity in it (Eccles. 5:18-20; 12:1; Heb. 4:1-4). A one-day rest of the week is a reminder to all of us that when work so dominates us, we have no time to cease from it. Restful contemplation is as essential as energetic activity in the worship and service of God (Ps. 46:10).

The writer of the Hebrews gives an argument on rest (ch.3,4). God rested when He completed the work of creation. God remains active. God remains active. The rest is not inactivity. It teaches that we rest from our own work by recognising our limitations and relying on God. The person who hears and obeys God's voice knows true rest.

'Sanctify' means 'to make holy.' God made the Sabbath a holy day because on that day He rested from all His work. 'Sanctifying the Sabbath' means that we praise the Creator. Human language cannot fully convey His greatness, glory and omnipotence. He deserves worship and praise from all His creatures. Sanctifying the day of the Lord is not just resting or hearing the word of God, but it is also turning to Him with all our hearts.[6]

He is holy and He demands that we be holy, too. He sanctifies individuals rather than days. Jesus accomplished what the Sabbath could not do: He created a new people and sanctified His followers. Jesus wants His followers to rest and to mediate on the privilege of being part of His new creation.

Celebrating Sunday

The early Christians no longer kept the Jewish Sabbath, rather they gathered together for fellowship with God and with one another on the first day of the week that is the Lord's Day. Sunday is not the continuation of or replacement for the Sabbath, it commemorates Jesus' resurrection on the first day of the week (John 20:1;19; Acts 20:7; 1 Cor. 16:2; Rev. 1:10). Sunday observance became the practice of each Church to meet weekly with one accord. Six of Jesus eight appearances took place on the first day of the week. Many think that the day of Pentecost was also Sunday. Sunday did not replace Saturday as if it were a Christian Sabbath to replace the Jewish Sabbath. But it points out the value of cessation from work and devotion to God.

There was no evidence for the transfer of the concept of a day of rest from Sabbath to Sunday. However, the Sabbath observance appeared in the Church and is reflected in the pronouncement of the fourth century council of Laodicea, that while, "Christians must not Judaise by resting on the Sabbath, they should, if possible, rest on the Lord's Day."[7] Jesus neither commanded us to keep Sunday, nor did He forbid us to keep the Sabbath. Man should not only worship God on Sabbath day or Sunday but on every day.

However, Sunday is a sign of Christ's victory that marks the new covenant. Justin Martyr, in AD 150, described the Church's worship "on the day called Sunday." Ignatius, also in the second century, says Christians 'have come to the possession of a new hope, no longer observing the Sabbath, but living in the observance of the Lord's day."[8] Besides giving us a rest from the stresses of the workweek, keeping the Sabbath day holy shows respect for God and reminds us to slow down our busy lives to give thanks to our Creator. Sunday is a day to look forward to, one when we get to enjoy the things that really matter.

On the day of the Lord, believers should joyfully spend more time with God. We should focus on God, for He is our Creator and Saviour. On this day, we should make a habit of reading the Bible more, hearing a good sermon and participating in prayer and worship. Modern-day Christians think that Sunday is a day to do whatever they want to do. Sunday, for Christians, should not be a holiday but a holy day.

Conclusion

The true God conceived the Sabbath rest for the benefit of all of humanity. Its existence yells out that there is a Being who not only exists, but who also cares deeply for His creation. The Sabbath gives a chance to our souls to catch up with our bodies to give a change to our souls through worship and meditation, to be enriched with new moral and spiritual values. This spiritual renewal that comes to us on the Sabbath through worship and meditation enables us to turn a new page in our life, to start a new week with a fresh provision of divine wisdom and grace

Notes

1. W. E. Vine, An Expository Dictionary of the New Testament Words, p.311.
2. Fleming H. Revell, The Revell Bible Dictionary, p.879.
3. J. D. Douglas, New Bible Dictionary, p.1043.
4. *Op.cit.*
5. *Op.cit.*
6. Abd Al-Masih, The Ten Commandments, p.90.

Honour Your Father and Mother

*Honour your father and your mother,
so that you may live long in the land the Lord
your God is giving you (Exod. 20:12).*

Introduction

The fifth commandment enjoins the honour of God's surrogate, parents to whom He grants a kind of co-creatorship in the begetting of children and to whom He grants a kind of co-rulership in the governing of children. Let any nation abandon respect for the mystery, dignity and authority of parenthood. Before long, the moral and social fabric of that nation is bound to disintegrate.

Loving one's parents and respecting them should be natural. Most people in all societies do. Entrenching respect for one's parents in a code of conduct may not seem particularly divine at all. Yet, a close analysis reveals that a divine mind is clearly behind this commandment as well.

All religions generally agree that parents ought to be honoured. It is natural for children to love and respect their parents. God protects the family with the fifth commandment. We should give thanks to God for the institution of family, its existence and its secret bonds of love and solidarity. In the fifth commandment, God commands us not only to honour our father just as the head of the family, but to love the mother and women in general. It is a uniquely stated commandment. The practical application of this commandment is to treat parents with respect. This is the first commandment with a promise (Eph. 6:2).

Honour

Honour, in general, means 'to be elevated' in the eyes of others on the basis of rank, reputation, status or character. It also means to respect a person in appropriate ways. The concept of honour in a unique way expresses a basic Christian attitude towards God, society and others as persons.

The word biblically means:

- Prize highly (Prov. 4:8).
- Care for (Ps. 91:15).
- Show respect for (Lev. 19:3; 20:9).
- Obey (Deut. 21:18-21).

"Honour is a decent respect to other persons, an inward esteem of them outwardly expressed upon all occasions in our conduct towards them. Fear them (Lev. 19:3), give them reverence (Heb. 12:9)."[1] Its contrary is mocking at them and despising them (Prov. 30:17).

"Honouring your father and your mother" is the understanding that parents are the representatives of God Himself. Our concept of God depends upon how we treat our parents. Honour means giving due respect and the dignity to our parents. It involves obedience and our deeper commitment to them. Even our consciences remind us to love and honour them because they are the most precious of all that we know or possess on earth.

Honour is shown by listening to and remaining open to their persuasion. Children must honour their parents by obedience; adult children should honour their parents by providing financial support (Eph. 6:1; 1 Tim. 5:8; Mark 7:9-13).

Parents

God demanded that parents be given the highest esteem. The punishment for not adhering to this commandment was stoning. Clearly, parents are very important in God's eyes. After a lifetime of suffering and sacrifices, God wants parents to be treated with the highest dignity, as a reward for their efforts. Respect for parents leads to the knowledge of God. Parents are to be honoured.

Another aspect that shows God's authorship of this commandment is the fact that parents are mentioned as deserving of reverence 'above' other authority figures. God knew all too well that, though most people would have treated the elderly with dignity, some would not have done so. Thus, the imposition of a commandment is with strong consequences, if transgressed.

If the Ten Commandments had been conceived by priests, they would have stressed 'their' dignity above that of parents, so as to reinforce their power and control. A priest-conceived code would have, logically, stressed the primary importance of the priesthood. They would have received primary emphasis in place of, or at least together with, parents; but they did not. Neither priests, *nor kings*, found a place within the Ten Commandments, because to God they did not have the same importance as parents. Respect for kings and priests was emphasised in the Book of the Law, but not in the 'Great Code.' This commandment is clearly from God.

Unfortunately, it is not what is happening in our society. An ever-increasing number of elderly people are being given over to old age homes to be looked after by strangers who do not always have their best interest at heart. It is also a very sad reality that the number of elderly who are being abused daily is scandalously high.

Father

Father is equivalent to *ab* in Hebrew and Pater in Greek. The father was legally responsible for his wife and children. A basic element in fatherhood is that it is related to origins, to bringing things into existence. People in biblical times used the word father in a respectful way.

In the Hebrew family, the father had absolute rights over the children. He could even send them into slavery and have them put to death (Lev. 18:21; 20:2-5; 2 Kings 23:10). To dishonour parents was a crime punishable with death (Exod. 21:15-17). He was also the chief religious functionary of the house, offering sacrifices to Jehovah on behalf of his family.² (Exod. 20:12; Lev. 19:3; Deut. 5:16).

Father is responsible for the education of his children (Prov. 22:6; Deut. 6:7-9), and to discipline his children wisely and lovingly (Prov. 13:24; Eph. 6:4; Heb. 12:2-11). He must provide for his family (Prov. 6:6-11; 1 Tim. 5:8). and to defend their rights in court. The Bible clearly instructs the father to have compassion for his children (Ps. 103:13). A father should demonstrate the spirit of Jesus and his integrity to his children, guide them in keeping His commandments and impress His promises upon their hearts.

Mother

Mother is equivalent to the Hebrew word *em*, and *Meter* in Greek. To the children, the mother was as worthy of honour as the father shown by the fifth commandment (Exod. 20:12). In Israel's culture, she prepared and cooked the food, carried the water, made clothing, worked with the men at harvest time and trained her daughters to do woman's work.

Mother is the female parent. Children are obligated to respect her (Exod. 20:12; Deut. 5:16; Matt. 15:4). A person who attacks his mother should be put to death (Exod. 21:15). She was an important partner with her husband in providing for the family (Prov. 31:10-31). We sense the tenderness associated with motherhood in the scripture.³

"Our mothers bore us for nine months, nearly 275 nights and days in their wombs. We were safe and provided for there. We shared her joy and anger, her sorrows and weariness. Perhaps our mothers prayed for us long before our birth. The act of our birth must have caused her much fear and pain."⁴

They took care of us day and night. They strove to provide us with food and clothing. They rejoiced with us and kept with us in our afflictions. Therefore, we must respect them.

Children

'Teknion' (GK) is a warm or affectionate 'dear child' or little child. In the Hebrew language, 'ben' means 'son' and 'bat' means daughter. Godly people regard their children as a gift from God (Ps. 127:3,4; Deut. 6:6-9, Eph. 6:4; 2 Tim. 3:15). Childlessness caused intense grief in the family (1 Sam. 1:1-16). Children must honour, obey and reverence their parents (Lev. 19:3; Deut. 5:16). Failure in these relations on the part of the child was a sin that could be punished by death (Deut. 21:18-28). The same high regard for parents is instructed to children in the New Testament (2 Cor. 12:14; Eph. 6:4; Col. 3:21). The Command to honour parents is found twice in the Old Testament (Deu. 5:16; Exod. 20:12) and six times in the New Testament.

The duties of the children to their parents are specified in this commandment. Children are submitted to the authority of the father. "A decent respect to their parents, an inward esteem of them outwardly expressed upon all occasion in our conduct towards them...The contrary to this is mocking at them and despising them."⁵ (Prov. 30:17). Fearing them and giving reverence are biblical (Lev. 19:3; Heb. 12:9). They must be obedient to the commands of their parents. It is natural for children to love and respect their parents.

God's Promise of Long Life

The fifth commandment is the first commandment with the promise (Eph. 6:2). The promise of long life is the annexe to this commandment. It offers children a clear promise of having a longer life by way of obeying their parents. "He who kindly takes care of His parents is promised a longer life on earth with less complaints and abundant blessings. When the parents' dignity is preserved, and where parents and children live in the ways of God, they will experience the fulfillment of this promise together."[6]

It is the uniquely stated commandment. There is a provisional clause (conditional) in it. "Honour your father and your mother…has a longer life." Those who build a society in which old age is honoured may themselves expect to enjoy similar treatment in their later years. At the beginning of human history, our ancestors lived more than nine hundred years, even up to nine hundred and sixty nine (Gen. 5:27); when disobedience started taking over the place of respect, the period of human life also started becoming short; and now the age of man (average, according to statistics) is forty-five only. Why? Respect for father and mother has been decreased in human history.

Family Is the Gift of God

The family is the nuclear unit of a husband, wife and their children. For 'family', there are two words in Hebrew, *Mishpaha* and *bayith*. *Patria* is the Greek word for it. In the Bible, the family was most commonly referred to as a house or household.

Stability, love and co-operation in the family help produce similar qualities in society as a whole. Parents must be careful that concern for the family's well-being does not make them or their children self-centred. The family is a place where people learn how to love, forgive honour and serve others. Such attitudes will help us develop godly character and produce a happy home within the family (Ps. 128:1-4; Eph. 4:31; Matt. 20:25-27).

God protects family with the fifth commandment. It is proper for us to give thanks to God for the institution of family, its existence and its secret bonds of love and solidarity. The nucleus family includes father, mother and children. The fifth commandment is concerned with all of them. "Family, then, is the nucleus of human life and the foundation of all cultures. It provides protection, security, and solidarity and often it proves to be far stronger than all the new ideologies."[7] All the members of a family are called to project the image of God and share the responsibilities with each other in the family and in society. If so, there will be no problem in the family.

Warning to Christians

God has given authority to parents over children; at the same time, the scripture warns parents against misuse of authority or unjust treatment of their children. Children are commanded to obey and respect their parents (Eph. 6:1-4; Col. 3:20-21). If parents will not instruct their children with much carefulness, they will remain ill-instructed or ill-disciplined. (Deut. 11:18-19; 2 Sam. 7:14-15; Prov. 1:8; Eph. 6:4; 1 Tim. 3:4,5; Heb. 12:7-11).

Parents are to provide for their children, to discipline and guide wisely and to communicate God's Word to them effectively (Exod. 12:26; Deut. 6:6,7). If parents train their children responsibly, they can expect from their children an exemplary life (Prov. 10:1,5). Such type of training should be carried out primarily in the home and is based on the word of God. (Deut. 6:6-9; 2 Tim. 3:14-15).

It is biblically a must for children to obey and respect their parents. Father and mother participated in the divine act of creation. The Lord honoured them by allowing them to deliver the genetic inheritance of generations to the infant within the mother. They watch our limbs and bodies grow, and respond to our agonies. In short, the Lord exhorts parents and children to observe watchfully this principle in the daily life of the family; especially to the children: "Honour your father and your mother" is the commandment.

Notes

1. Mathew Henry's Commentary, p.125.
2. Merril C.Tenny, Zondervan Pictorial Bible Dictionary, pp.276-279.
3. Fleming H. Revell, The Revell Bible Dictionary, p.712.
4. Abd al-Masih, The Ten Commandments, p.109.
5. Mathew Henry's Commentary, p.125.
6. *Op.Cit.*, pp.114-15.
7. *Ibid.*, p.107.

No Murder

You shall not murder (Exod. 20:13).

Introduction

The sixth commandment is a prohibition of murder. The life of every human person has worth and value. We are to actively protect and guard one another. A man's life is his utterly indispensable possession, but more than that, man is God's image bearer. Murder destroys God's image. So, capital punishment is the penalty affixed to a breaking of this law.

God is the creator of human beings. He is the life-giver. The solemn authority of the Lord guards our lives. The sovereignty is upon the Lord over the lives of humankind. As the Lord is the owner and sustainer of our lives, no one is permitted to kill himself (suicide) or someone else (murder).

Define the Term

There were two words for murder in the Hebrew language: (1) *rasah* (personal killings) and (2) *haraq* (other killings). The word *rasah* is used in the sixth commandment (Exod. 20:13). It prohibits only personal killing. It does not refer to war or capital punishment, or killing other living creatures. There are few words in Greek for murder. *Anaireo* and *apokteino* are the general terms that simply affirm that someone has been deprived of his or her life. (Matt. 10:28; Heb. 10:9). These terms were used to point out killing physically or metaphorically. *Thanato*, to put to death, is translated as 'are killed' in Rom. 8:36. *Diacheirizo* is used primarily in the sense of laying hands on with a view to kill or of actually killing (Acts 5:30). *Phoneuo* is the best word used in the New Testament, as same as *rasah* in the Old Testament. *Phoneuo* means murder (Matt. 5:21; Luke 18:20). Wherever this word occurs, the act of killing is viewed as wicked and intentional. Phoneus (murderer), *Anthropoktonos* (manslayer) and *patroloas* (murderer of one's father) are also used in the scripture. (1 Peter 4:15; John. 8:44; 1 Tim. 1:9).[1]

'Murder' is an act of killing a human being with pre-meditated malice. It denotes killing in a barbarous or inhuman manner. Murder is the unlawful and intentional killing of one human being by another. It is the personal and intentional killing of another human being, in contrast to accidental homicide or causing the death of another person in war or in defense of one's property.

Within the Middle Eastern societies of the time, murder must have been very common. The wounding of the family's honor could not be by-passed and forgotten, if the respect of the community was to be retained. Alcohol abuse must have abounded as well as the mortal conflicts that often ensue from drunkenness. Knives and swords were not forbidden, and, therefore, their use must have been quite common.

The ancient world was a fierce world. Self-control and rational thinking were not necessarily stressed or taught. Pride, instead, was taught and nurtured. Offended males would teach the offender a lesson by reacting violently and vengefully; escalation would, no doubt, regularly ensue, and death would have followed often. God said to Israel that the time had come for self-control and respect for the lives of others. Killing another human being out of anger, pride, etc., would be no longer tolerated. Penalty: death.

Murder in the Old Testament

The first man born of a woman (Cain) and loved by his father was the murderer of his brother. The Bible exposes this crime and the corruption rooted deeply and mercilessly in the human heart. Every man carries, by nature, the hereditary qualities of a murderer within himself. If someone appears to be stronger, wiser, more godly, or more beautiful, he envies him and hates him. In Semitic culture, murder is an unpardonable crime and it cannot be atoned for except by the shedding of the murderer's blood, or that of his substitute.

The Semitic custom of the avenger of the blood was: The murdered man's nearest relative had the duty to pursue the slayer and kill him. (Num. 35:19). The Mosaic Law provided for cities of refuge for a man, pursued by the avenger of blood, could flee (Num. 35). He would be admitted and tried; if judged guilty of murder, he would be turned over to the avenger; if judged innocent, he was afforded protection in this city from the avenger. In a murder trial, the agreeing testimony of at least two persons was necessary for conviction. (Num. 35:30; Deut. 17:6). An animal known to be vicious had to be confined and if it caused the death of anyone, the animal was to be destroyed and the owner held guilty of murder (Exod. 21:29,31). If the murderer could not be found, the people of the community where the dead body was found were reckoned guilty. To clear them of guilt, the elders of that place would kill a heifer, wash their hands over it and state their innocence and thus be judged clean (Deut. 21:1-9).

Murder refers to unauthorised killing. This law is amplified with reference to accidental and therefore excusable (Exod. 21:13; Num. 35) and justifiable (Exod. 22:2) homicide. Capital punishment is authorised killing (Gen. 9:6) and so is lawful war (Deut. 20).

Punishment

As the other commandments, this one, too, went against the culture and psychological mental sets of the times. Historians tell us that other major pieces of legal code of the time did not regard murder as a crime of concern to the State. It is worth noting that neither the Code of Hammurabi or the Middle Assyrian Laws have any general provisions on murder... murder was not treated as a crime but as a matter for the relatives of the deceased.' Protecting the honour of the family was a duty of the family as was getting revenge for the murder of a family member.

The death sentence in the Old Testament was issued as a deterrent and a fulfillment of justice against every murderer and assassin (Exod. 21:12,14,18). God's law makes careful distinction regarding murder. An accidental killing is treated differently from a premeditated or intentional killing. To exact the death penalty in ancient Israel, the judges had to establish a motive (hostility, intent) and determine that the means used (the weapon, the method) led directly to the victim's death (Num. 35 ch.). As a further safeguard, these elements were to be proven on the testimony of witness. But no one is to be put to death on the testimony of only one witness. (Num. 35:30).

The person convicted of intentional *rasah* under these standards was to be put to death. But if without hostility, someone suddenly shoves another or drops a stone on him that could kill him and he dies, if he did not intend to harm him, the assembly must protect the one accused of murder (Num. 35:22-25).

However, the law that lay down the death penalty for murderers was based on a command that God gave long before the nation Israel existed. God's command was related to the fundamental sacredness of human life, for man exists in God's image. Therefore, God laid down the law that any person was no longer fit to enjoy God's gift of life. (Gen. 9:3-6; cf Exod. 21:23; Num. 35:30-34).[2]

Abortion

Abortion is a type of killing. The debate over this issue is admittedly complex. All Christians believe that the Almighty God is the only giver, sustainer and taker away of life. On the one hand, 'He Himself gives all men life and breath and everything else; on the other, as the Psalmist says to God, 'when you take away their breath, they die and return to the dust.'

To the Christian, both life-giving and life-taking are purely the works of God. Terminating a human life is the height of arrogance. Abortion is the most devilish thing that a human hand can do. It is a terrible sin. If a man steps forward to abort, he is killing life. Everybody agrees that the embryo is living and human. The present practice reflects a rejection of the biblical view of divine sovereignty and human dignity. If so, a deeply committed Christian cannot stand aside from its debate.³

Since the life of the human fetus is a human life, with the potential of becoming a mature being, we have to learn to think of mother and unborn child as two human beings at different stages of development. The Bible has dealt with God's special concern for the defenseless and, I should say, the most defenseless of all people are unborn children. Satan is the child specialist and the specialist for abortion. Satan is trying his level best to kill a number of unborn children. They are speechless to plead their own cause and helpless to protect their own life. So it is our responsibility to do for them what they cannot do for themselves. You shall not murder, in this sense, means, "you shall not abort."

Suicide

Suicide is a tragic act of killing oneself. Suicide is self-murder. If a Christian should not murder somebody else, he or she must not murder himself or herself. We are created in the image of God. As He has given us life, it is under His authority to determine when it is going to end. (Job. 1:21; 1 Cor. 6:19).

Suicide has been condemned inferentially in the Bible. The Bible gives some very definite guidelines on how to live our lives, even though the word 'suicide' is not mentioned in the Bible. We see some examples of suicide: King Saul (1 Sam. 31:4-5), Ahitophel (2 Sam. 17:23) Zimri (1 Kings 16:18), and Judas Iscariot (Matt. 27:5). Some scholars say that Samson's heroic death is a case of approved suicide (Judg. 16:30).

There are different types of suicide:

- **Mass Suicide:** An entire group or a small community entering into a pact and committing suicide

- **Egoistic Suicide:** An individual, thinking of nothing else and nobody else but his or her own misery or pain, commits suicide.

- **Self-denial:** It indicates the self-sacrifice of one's life for someone else who is in danger or for a cause.

- **Attempted Suicide:** If a suicide attempt is not successful, it is called attempted suicide.[4]

Suicide is a rejection of God's sovereignty over life and an attack upon the sanctity of life. Killing one's self is a grave sin. Suicide is an immoral or unethical action; therefore, it can never be justified. It is an act of self-destruction. 'You shall not commit suicide' is included in the sixth commandment.

The Christian Perspective

Murder does not have to be necessarily a physical act in the light of the New Testament. Jesus taught that murder can also be done with the heart or mind. The Bible says that whosoever hates his brother is a murderer. Hating equates killing before the eyes of the Lord. Murder can even be committed with the tongue, according to the Book of James.

If someone treats others badly, not caring if they go hungry and does not warn them against impending future, he also falls under the category of murderer. If anyone wounds a person, puts poison in his food or encourages somebody else to kill him, he will sit with all killers on a bench of eternal judgment. If anyone harms another and thereby shortens his life, he is also a murderer according to the Bible (Rom. 13:1-18). God holds us accountable for our fellowmen.[5]

Jesus calls the devil 'a murderer from the beginning', for he removed man from his original fellowship with God and caused him to die (John 8:44). Ever since, death has controlled humankind, for 'the wages of sin is death.' Humans have many motives and reasons for killing. Jesus reveals that the intention to murder is the first of all evil thoughts that come out of men's hearts (Matt. 15:19). But the Lord opposed man's evil intent and forbade him to carry out his devastating aims through the sixth commandment. The evil thoughts have to be removed from our hearts and replaced with new thoughts. Therefore, all kinds of killing are against the will of God and considered as nothing less than open rebellion against God Himself.

In His Sermon on the Mount, Jesus teaches us that not only killing the body, but also slander is considered to be murder. It can have a long-term effect like poison. Any kind of slander, hateful lies, deliberate threats, bitter strife, intentional cursing and betrayal of trust or mockery are spiritually deadly. They poison first the heart of the one who speaks these words, then they poison the mind of the accused. Therefore, murder does not have to be a physical act. Jesus taught that murder can also be done with the heart or the mind (Matt. 5:22). Whosoever hates his brother is a murderer (1 John 3:15). Slander, deliberate threats, etc., can be signified "character assassination" or 'verbal assassination.'

Jesus said, "You have heard that it was said to those of old, "you shall not murder" and whosoever murders will be in danger of the judgment. But I say unto you that whoever is angry with his brother without a cause shall be in danger of the judgment. And anyone who says to his brother, *Raca*, is answerable to the Sanhedrin. But anyone who says, 'you fool' will be in danger of the fire of hell" (Matt. 5:21,22). Through this statement, Jesus declared us all to be guilty and judged us as evil-hearted people with a murderous spirit, who deserve eternal condemnation in hell. We should repent and acknowledge that we all have murderous thoughts in our hearts. Anger, envy, persistence in hateful disputes, a vengeful spirit, cruelty and brutality are emotions and acts that assail not just adults, but also children.

We should examine ourselves honestly. Otherwise, these bad thoughts can take root in our hearts and demoralise us. Our willingness to forgive will help us to conquer every hatred and our decision to forgive will overcome our desire to destroy our enemies. For this reason, Jesus bore our sins and carried the punishment on our behalf (Isa. 53). Jesus bore our sins and the sins of all mockers and murderers. That is why we have the privilege of forgiving everyone's sins without exception. Jesus said, "But I tell you love your enemies; pray for those who persecute you, that you may be sons of your Father in heaven" (Matt. 5:44,45).

Conclusion

The sixth commandment is the prohibition against killing, which has to do only with the unlawful shedding of blood by an individual and not with killing done by the community either in the form of the death penalty or of war.

If this were a man-invented principle, humans would have resisted it and, eventually, heavily modified or abolished it. If an all-powerful God stood behind it, it would have stood and become an authoritative, unchangeable commandment—and it did.

Notes

1. W. E. Vine, An Expository Dictionary of New Testament Words, 1966, p.92.

2. Don Fleming, Bible Knowledge Dictionary, 1990, p.122.

3. John Stott, Issues Facing Christians Today, 1984, p.280

4. Emmanuel E. James, Ethics: A Biblical Perspective, 1992, p.227.

5. Abd Al-masih, The Ten Commandments, p.122.

No Adultery

You shall not commit adultery (Exod. 20:14).

Introduction

Adultery abounds in our society. It abounded in ancient societies as well. In ancient times, men had no compunction about lusting after married women; they had no scruples about taking advantage of them, if possible. God, being a moral Being, concerned with family unity and with preventing psychological traumas in betrayed mates and children, commanded, 'Thou shalt not commit adultery.'

The seventh commandment is a prohibition of adultery that safeguards the sanctity of marriage and creates a boundary around home. If anyone goes beyond this boundary, we see nowadays that such home will be undermined by marital infidelity. God does not regard sexual love in marriage as unclean or impure, but blessed and holy as long as man lives faithfully to his one partner. Sexual love and desire are given to preserve the reverent marital relationship with the intention of having children by the grace of God.

Defining Adultery

For the term adultery, *naap* is used in the Hebrew and *moicheia* in Greek. It is a specific sexual sin forbidden in both Testaments. "Adultery *(naap)* is a sexual relationship with a married person who is not one's spouse."[1]

Adultery is a sexual contact between a married person and someone other than that person's marriage partner. But fornication is a sexual relation between two people who are not married.[2] (Exod. 20:14; Rom. 12:9,20; Gal. 5:19; 1 Thess. 4:3-4). Adultery is a sin against one's own marriage partner (Mal. 2:11,14, Hos. 2:2). Unfaithfulness is at the centre of all adultery. The prophets of the Old Testament repeatedly spoke of Israel's unfaithfulness to God as spiritual adultery or spiritual prostitution (Jer. 5:7; 23:10; Ezek. 16:30-38, 23:4-5; Hos. 9:1).

The term 'adultery' has to do with any kind of sexual activity outside the heterosexual marriage bed. Living together outside of marriage is a sin. God warns His people against immorality.

Adultery in the Old Testament

The seventh commandment concerns our own and our neighbour's chastity. For our chastity should be as dear to us as our lives and we should be as much afraid of that which defiles the body. It is a sin against God (Gen. 39:9) and against the marriage partner.

In ancient Israel, it was important to maintain one's virginity up to the time of marriage (Deut. 22:13-22). Fornication by a person engaged to be married was treated as adultery (Deut. 22:22-27). Unengaged people who had sexual relations were to marry, unless the girl's parents objected (Exod. 22:16-17; Deut. 22:28-29).

According to the Mosaic Law, a wife suspected of adultery be brought before the priest. A rigorous ceremonial procedure followed, which would clear or condemn her (Num. 5:11-31). The Old Testament Law demands the death penalty for adultery, indicating how serious this sin is before the Lord (Lev. 18:20; 20:10; Deut. 22:22-24). The punishment for adultery was death by stoning[3] (Lev. 20:10; John 8:3-5). The one exception is that of a woman who had been raped (Deut. 22:22-27). There are terrible penalties that come with adultery. The Lord warns us about the danger of such potent activity; that is why God hates it so.

Perverted Sex

Sexual intercourse is considered appropriate only within marriage. Some sins of perverted sex are mentioned in the scripture ranging from premarital intercourse (fornication) to prostitution, rape, homosexuality, bestiality, polygamy, adultery, etc. God condemns them as perversions (Lev. 18:6-18; 19:29; 20:10-21; Rom. 1:26-27; 1 Cor. 6:9-10. 1 Tim. 1:9-10; Rev. 21:8). The union of a man and a woman to become 'one' means that it excludes all others (Gen. 2:24; Matt. 19:5,6). The scripture encourages a healthy enjoyment of sex with the partner (Prov. 5:18-19; Eccles. 9:9; Song of Sol. 7:6-13) but it forbids pre-marital sex, and adultery is extra-marital sex.

Polygamy is unscriptural. Notice that God created one woman for one man, not more than one for the other partner. Having more than one wives or husbands is a sin against God's order. The transgressors suffered the consequences of their sins (Lev. 20:10; Deut. 22:22-26). God's ideal of monogamy is best. Jesus also confirmed monogamy (Matt. 19:4-6; Gen. 21:8-10; Judg. 8:30 f.; 2 Sam. 3:2-5; Deut. 21:15-17).

Homosexuality is a sin in the sight of God (Gen. 19:1-10). Men with men and women with women in sexual activity is an abomination to the Creator.[4] God punishes such people. Men and women having sexual intercourse with animals will also be punished with death. No form of sexual intercourse is permitted by God except in the framework of marriage between husband and wife.

Sex-crazed societies of the past, where temple worship often entailed sexual relations with priestesses and temple prostitutes, would have had no respect for a human commandment that would forbid sexual freedom—if humans had concocted it, that is. No human in his right mind would interfere with the sexual freedom desired by the masses, especially in the Middle East where sexual perversions abounded (Deut. 18:9-14). God intervened because He could see the agony that accompanies adultery, the problems that ensued illegitimate births

Since the Sixties, the Western world has adopted a *laissez faire* mentality toward sex and the results have been horrific. While before men were the ones that betrayed their wives, the trend now is for both to explore the excitement of having an affair. Such an irresponsible and hedonistic approach to marriage has made thousands susceptible to incurable venereal diseases that then bring devastating viruses to innocent and unknowing mates. The scourge of AIDS is presently decimating Sub-Saharan

Africa. Whole nations run the risk of disappearing within the next twenty years because of sexual irresponsibility. The same scourge is spreading through the rest of the world and will continue to in spite of the superficial and ineffective safe sex campaigns.

The New Testament Teaching on Adultery

Jesus quotes the commandment (Matt. 5:27-30; 19:18; Mark 10:19; Luke 18:20). He broadened its application to include the lustful look that destroys an adulterous heart. He teaches that such evils as adultery come from the heart (Matt. 15:19; Matt. 7:21). Having desire for unlawful sexual relations is a form of adultery. Therefore, we should avoid the adulterous thoughts first (Matt. 5:27-30; James 1:14,15). Here Jesus shifts the focus from acts to inner intent.

In John 8:2-11, a woman taken in adultery reveals Jesus' insistence on the equal guilt of the man. He did not underestimate the seriousness of adultery; at the same time, Jesus exercises the sovereign pardoning power of the grace of God. "Adultery is wrong and a person committing this sin falls short of being righteous. But to fix one's gaze on another person and engage in sexual fantasies is also wrong and shows just as clearly that the person who look lustfully is not righteous either."[5]

Paul the Apostle quotes the commandment (Rom. 13:9). He pointed out that all Christians should avoid all immoral sexual relations because the Holy Spirit dwells in them (1 Cor. 6:13-20). Adultery is the work of the flesh and adulterers will not inherit the kingdom of God (Gal. 5:19; 1 Cor. 6:9). The sanctity of marriage is stressed in the scripture (Heb. 13:4;

James 2:11). Paul used it as an analogy of our relation to God (Rom. 7:3).

The New Testament treatment of adultery is that all sexual impurity is sin against God, against self and against others. The spiritual adulterer violates the union between Christ and His own. The New Testament announces God's judgment on those who are immoral and adulterous (Heb. 13:4; 2 Pet. 2:14). At the same time, Jesus gives forgiveness to those who come to Him, leaving the sinful ways and asking pardon for the sins they committed (1 Cor. 6:9-11; Matt. 9:11-13; John 8:3-11; Rom. 2:22).

Adulterous thought start in the mind. Our mind pictures seductive images that entangle us in a deadly web. Gradually, we put these dreams into action and deliberately commit sin. When the desire increases, the heart will be silenced and hardened to the extent that it becomes a habit. Whoever commits sin is a slave to sin (John 8:34). If anyone who committed sin asks for pardon, Jesus can cleanse and heal him completely. The blood of Jesus Christ cleanses from all sins and empowers His children to overcome temptations. The forgiveness of sins by the blood of Jesus grants us a comforted soul, a purified body, and creates a fresh atmosphere in our lives. We should be ready to live according to the values of believers in Jesus Christ, who have inherited His purity and His holiness.

Marriage and Divorce

God created man and woman in the image of God. He grants both partners one mind and one goal and makes them equal spiritually. The Lord binds two selfish people together with the intention of helping them to overcome their selfishness by His gentle and kind spirit. Marriage was distorted as soon as both partners strayed away from their fellowship with God. Woman and man wanted to be like God. This temptation distorted all aspect of life. Consequently, men began to take several wives, which created several problems for them.

The Old Testament identify adultery as grounds for divorce; while it is likely that unfaithfulness caused some to divorce, there is biblical record of this. It might be due to the law of Lev. 20:10, which established death by stoning as the penalty for adultery[6] (Deut. 22:22-30). Dealing with divorce, Jesus declares remarriage of a divorced man or woman to be adultery (Matt. 5:31,32; 19:3-9; Matt. 10:2-12; Luke 16:18). But the only exception that Jesus allowed concerned the case where persistent adulterous behaviour by one partner had already virtually destroyed the marriage (Matt. 5:32; 19:7-9). Jesus brands divorce and marriage as adultery. He said that a man should not put as under what God has joined. The ideal union of family will be broken only by death, in which the surviving partner is free to remarry (Rom. 7:2-3; 1 Cor. 7:39; 1 Tim. 5:14).

Warnings to Christians

Christians should avoid all immoral sexual relations because they themselves belong to Christ. Some people may not even feel shame or sinful in their sexual misbehaviour (Eph. 4:19; 1 Pet. 4:3-4; 2 Pet. 2:12-14). It should not be tolerated by Christians. The Church should remove from its fellowship those who openly reject God's standards (1 Cor. 5:1-5;11). Christians should control their thoughts and deeds and avoid temptation.

God condemns prostitution, bestiality, incest, and homosexual practices as perversions (Lev. 18:6–18; 1 Cor. 6:9–10; Rev. 21:8). Prostitutes bring lasting damage to themselves and their lovers. The Bible gives strong warnings against them (Prov. 2:16–19; 5:1–14; 6:23–27); penalty for it was death (Lev. 19:29; Deut. 22:21; John 8:5).

Those who treat sexual intercourse as no more than a physical function reduce themselves to the level of animals. They deny the dignity that God has given them (Rom. 1:24–27). If people will feel sorry for their sexual misconduct, having turned from it and ask God's forgiveness, they can be assured that the Lord and His Church will forgive (Matt. 9:12–13; John 8:10,11; 1 Cor. 6:9–11; 2 Cor. 2:7; Gal. 6:1–2; Heb. 8:12).

The commandment forbidding adultery was meant to spare untold suffering for hundreds of millions who will die excruciating and needless deaths. It was also meant to spare hundreds of innocent children the agony of seeing their parents die and be left to fend for themselves in horrendous circumstances. A Supreme Divine Mind who is concerned deeply about us all uttered this commandment.

Conclusion

Each person must be loyal to his or her spouse, thus mirroring the covenant commitment that exists between God and his people. The teaching of the Bible is that sexual relations are lawful only between husband and wife. Human sexuality is a gift of God. People can properly use and enjoy it or abuse it shamefully. Sexual relations outside the marriage bond are regarded in the Old Testament and the New Testament as immoral.

Objective and aware minds see the critical value of this commandment. The family unit is critical if a society is to remain healthy and strong. Strong, loving families make for healthy minds and have an anti-deviant effect on the minds of future adults. God knew of the devastating impact that adultery, and ensuing divorce, would have on society and on individuals and intervened to keep it from happening.

Notes

1. Fleming H. Revell, Revell Bible Dictionary, p.25.
2. Don Fleming, Bible knowledge Dictionary, p.9.
3. *Ibid.*
4. Dan Betzer, The Ten Commandments, p.24.
5. Fleming H. Revell, Revell Bible Dictionary, p.26.
6. *Ibid.*

No Stealing

You shall not steal (Exod. 20:15).

Introduction

The eighth commandment is a prohibition of theft in any and all forms. Property is essentially an extension of a man's personality, and thus this law indicates that the rights and achievements of one's neighbour must not be ignored. Our special concern for others must extend to honouring their property. We are to love others, not use them for material gain.

The Bible clearly says, "You shall not steal", thereby affirming private property. Therefore, we should not envy someone's riches, for his eternal responsibility increases with his wealth. The wealth of the rich cannot justify stealing from them, because everyone who steals bears the judgement of God.

Terminology

The Hebrew word for stealing is *gannav*. The Greek word *Klepto* means to steal. *Kleptes* means a thief (Matt. 6:19,20; Mark 10:19). The word *Kleptes* is used literally (Matt. 24:43), metaphorically

(John 10:8) and figuratively for false teachers (Rev. 3:3). Another word *Lestes* is frequently rendered *thieves* (Matt. 21:13). There are some other words in Greek for theft: (1) *Klope* = to steal. It is used in the plural in Matt. 15:19; Mark 7:22; (2) *Klemma* = a thing stolen. It is also used in the plural in Rev. 9:21.[1]

Stealing is an act of taking another's property secretly, illegally or without permission. The one who steals secretly and without violence is a thief. A thief takes the property of another. Although some thieves used violence (John 10:10), most used surprise 'to break in and to steal' (Matt. 6:19; Exod. 22:2). Stealing is an offense. There is a sanction that God gives to private property. Appropriating a person's property against his will is a sin. The motive behind it is beside the point.

Stealing is that the thief unlawfully takes what belongs to someone else. Covetousness and greed are usually the cause of stealing (Mic. 2:2; James. 1:14-15; 4:1-2). Stealing is wrong regardless of the reason. As stealing is taking or obtaining from another, without right or permission in subtle manner, it is immoral. It is an evil practice of the ungodly.

The Bible on Stealing

Under the Law of Moses, thieves who were caught were expected to restore twice the amount stolen. Exod. 22:1-4 is the biblical portion of Mosaic Law that is in connection with the protection of property. It is the prohibition against stealing. Stealing is a scheduled sin that welcomes severe punishment. It is one of the Ten Commandments (Exod. 20:15). It is the eighth in the order of Decalogue.

Achan was an Israelite who had stolen a garment, some silver and some gold. By a process of elimination, Achan was found out. Although he confessed, all Israel stoned him. They raised over him a great heap of stones (Josh. 6:17-19; 7:25-26). He was found guilty of theft what God has forbidden.

There are many reasons why people steal. For some people, stealing is part of their way of life and they may even have deliberately set out on a path of robbery and violence (Judg. 9:25). For others, stealing is contrary to their normal behaviour, but they may have been overcome by temptation in a moment of weakness (Josh.7:21). Coveteousness and greed are usually the cause of stealing (Mic. 2:2). Some people steal because they are poor and in desperate need (Prov. 30:8-9). A hungry man who steals food is not as bad as a lustful man who steals another's wife (Prov. 6:30-35). Through deceit and cunning, they cheat and exploit the defenseless, but any dishonesty in such matters is still a form of stealing (1 Kings 21:1-15; Prov. 21:6; Isa.1:23, Mic. 6:10-13).[2]

Malachi's classic query is to be also discussed (3:8). We can rob God by failure to tithe. Tithe is 10 percent of our gross income. Tithe belongs to our local church and not to any para-church organisation. Failure to tithe is to rob God. Therefore, "you shall not rob God."

Jesus Christ explained who is the thief and what is stealing. The purpose of stealing is also explained in the gospels. "The thief comes only to steal and kill and destroy; I have come that they may have life and have it to the full" (John 10:10). Although Jesus has mentioned here the works of Satan, it is easier for us to understand the works of a thief. He also said that Satan is a liar and the father of lies (John 8:44). Jesus said that we shall not lay up for ourselves treasures on earth because thieves break in and steal (Matt. 6:19).

Judas, who betrayed our Lord, was a thief and in charge of the treasury (John 12:6). He hanged himself in the end. The two thieves who died on crosses next to Jesus were probably highwaymen, who attacked and killed or injured their victims and thus deserved the death penalty imposed upon them (Luke 23:41).

Paul the apostle clearly said that thieves, the greedy, etc., will not inherit the kingdom of God (1 Cor. 6:10). If we do not train our conscience in the uprightness of the Holy Spirit, we will be in danger of losing our righteousness and salvation through greed for money and envy of property. The following verse applies to every Christian: "He who has been stealing must steal no longer but must work, doing something useful with his own hands that he may have something to share with those in need" (Eph. 4:28). Paul worked diligently with his own hands. He did not want to impose himself on others. If we live under God's guidance and work diligently, we do not need to steal or live off others, because we will not only be blessed to support our families, but can help the needy and participate with our prayerful sacrifices in the Lord's work as well (Acts 20:35; Eph. 4:28; 1 Thess. 4:11).

Punishment

Those found guilty of stealing should make repayment to the lawful owner as well as pay the legal penalty (Exod. 20:15;

22:1ff). If a person steals a cow, for example, the Bible says he should not only give the cow back, but buy his victim a second cow. We can think of it as a hundred per cent penalty. Some other biblical cases of restitution demand five hundred per cent payback.

Humans have taken what is not theirs since time began. Most stealing is done secretly. A man can steal secretly, in great abundance, and for long periods of time, and yet retain a semblance of dignity and honesty. God speaks to these types, and to all of us, with total authority: No stealing is allowed, or one will have to answer to the 'All-Seeing Ruler' (Ezek. 22:29-31).

Jesus has provided a better way to overcome stealing. He did not abolish the nation's penalties for stealing. Instead, He bore the penalty of eternal punishment on Himself and atoned for everyone who stole. When a person becomes Christian, out of his gratitude for the Lord's painful suffering and sacrifice, he will never touch anything that is not his. The spirit of truth will set everyone free from the spirit of theft.

If a thief becomes Christian, God will punish him no more. As he will become a blood-washed saint in Christ and being set free from the spirit of theft, he is responsible to despise the old evil practices. But he must not be satisfied simply with correcting the past and deciding to earn an honest living in the future. He must have the added goal of giving generously to those in need (Eph. 4:28).

Modern Stealing

It would be better to think of various forms of stealing that are being observed today in many lives. It is not just taking away the things that do not belong to us but also embezzlement, procrastination and wasting time at work. Stealing can involve more than burglary or filching. Stealing can mean borrowing without any intention of returning or repaying. Stealing can involve leaving bills unpaid. According to Dan Betzer, vandalism is also stealing. We see that public buildings are defaced, windows shattered and lawns torn up. Christians ought not to do these things because they could be enlisted to the act of stealing.[3]

Every form of cheating is stealing. Selling defective items expensively is cheating. Turning in wrong information to tax administration is also stealing. It is theft for banks and individuals if they ask for high interest rates. In modern society, stealing has taken various forms. If we take what we see in a shop and do not pay for it, we become thieves.[4] There are many ways to cheat at work and in economic dealings, both private and public. Do not forget that envy and greed are the root causes of all evil. If we labour for money, our hearts will get hardened, our love will grow cold and everything we do will be out of a desire for money. If money becomes the focus of our life, God is no longer at the centre. We must be sure that we do not make money-making the supreme goal of our life, or become materialistic and lose the joy of the Lord.

Duty of a Christian

A Christian, however, should realise that property belongs to the Creator and that nothing belongs to us. We are not owners or independent masters, but humble stewards only. What we have is just a blessing from God and we have to give an account of how we use our money, time and effort. Jesus has endowed his followers with a new heart in which meaningful life is not seen in terms of money, possessions and comfort; but in spiritual life, whose bond is love, service and gratitude.

Wealthy Christians should not plan and live for themselves, but actually ask God what He wants them to do with the money He has entrusted to them. A Christian believer looks at the poor with love and compassion and plans to help them so that they may grow responsible for themselves and work honestly and diligently. At the same time, many new believers should change their attitude to money and learn to work honestly, because begging or waiting for help from others is not honourable and does not secure adequate income. The fourth request in the Lord's Prayer, "Give us this day our daily bread" also means that we pray confidently to our heavenly father to give us a proper job and bless us with health.[5]

Our conscience is very sensitive and warns us not to steal anything, big or small. We should ask Jesus to give us courage to return what is not ours immediately. We need to ask God and the owners for forgiveness and remission. Stolen things will affect our conscience and destroy our relationship with Jesus. Therefore, the Lord commands all of us: "You shall not steal".

Conclusion

God conceived of this command because He is a God of justice. God cares deeply for the innocent victims who often have their life savings snatched by arrogant, callous criminals. He is a Father who wants humans to show respect for one another and to treat others as they want to be treated. Such is undeniable evidence of *divine* love.

Notes

1. W. E. Vine, An Expository Dictionary of New Testament Words, 1966, pp.72, 126.
2. Don Fleming, Bible Knowledge Dictionary, p.419.
3. Dawn Betzer, The Ten Commandments, 1990, p.27.
4. Abd al-Masih, The Ten Commandments, p.164.
5. *Ibid.*, p.166.

No False Testimony

You shall not give false testimony against your neighbour (Exod. 20:16).

Introduction

The ninth commandment is a prohibition of falsehood in its many varieties. Truth is the cement of community. The scripture stresses the need for a sanctified tongue. We are to guard other's reputation, lives and property.

This commandment prohibits lying. God is really angered by lying. Lying is the characteristic that most closely identifies with Satan. Satan is the father of lies. Lying is the sin that is contrary to the nature of God. God lumps liars with the heathen, the abominable, murderers, whoremongers, sorcerers and idolaters. God does not slander or betray; He is not tricky and does not deceive. He is pure and His word is true. He urges us to speak the truth in love.

Testimony or Witness

Testimony and witness are interchangeably used in the scripture. *Martureo* is the Greek word used for witness, which is frequently rendered to bear witness. It is to 'testify' in Authorised version and to 'witness' in Revised version (John 2:25; 1 Cor. 15:15; Heb. 7:17). *Marturion* is a testimony or witness.[1] (Acts 4:33; James 5:3).

Testimony is to give evidence at legal proceeding of what one has seen or learned about (Lev. 5:1; Deut. 8:19). Testifying means giving evidence for or against a person or speaking out as a witness to some spiritual reality (Jer. 14:7; John 5:32-36). In short, testimony is the evidence given by a witness (probably in the court) (Deut. 17:6). Witness is a person who gives testimony concerning something about which he has personal knowledge (Deut. 19:15; Acts 1:8) It was commonly used to refer to a person who saw, knew or experienced something (Deut. 17:6; Acts. 5:30-32) or to that person's open declaration of what he saw, knew or experienced. His witness was his testimony (Exod. 20:16; John 3:11).[2] Witness was used to denote that person's oath or guarantee of the truth (Acts 10:33; Rom. 3:21) and a person who swore to the truth of something (Ruth. 4:9; 1 Sam. 12:5; 2 Cor. 1:23).

As far as the Law is concerned, the main requirement was that there be at least two witnesses if the judges were to accept or act upon any accusation (Deut. 19:15; Matt. 18:15-16). The Law required the witness to participate publicly in the punishment, if the accused was found guilty (Deut. 17:6-7). It was to discourage people from making accusations secretly or lightly. Early commercial transactions were also conducted in front of witnesses who could testify later to any conditions (Gen. 23; Ruth. 4:9). Later, written contracts served this purpose (Jer. 32:11,12).

False Testimony

Various Hebrew words portray falsehood and deceit in the Old Testament. These words emphasise four aspects:[3]

1. Falsehood has no basis in reality.

2. The false is empty, unreal.

3. The false violates commitments.

4. The false is undependable.

There are 15 different Greek words expressing the idea of falsehood in the New Testament. Most built on the root 'pseudo.' 'Pseudomai' means of them 'to deceive by lying.' It is in contrast to God's revelation of truth as an accurate portrayal of reality. Man's rejection of divine revelation has led humanity into a world of falsehood and illusion.

God's revealed word is the standard by which we measure what is true and false. We are called to be true in our own lives and relationship with others. Falsehood draws our attention to the difference between reality and illusion. Only God knows reality as it truly is. Therefore, we should deepen our understanding of what is true and trustworthy.

If a witness has sufficient evidences to present, he must not be silent (Lev. 5:1), but if the judges find the witness guilty of giving false testimony, they should inflict upon him the punishment that he should bring upon the accused (Deut. 19:16–21; Mark 14:55–56). The Law is very strict with false witnesses and accusations. If a witness's testimony is proved to be false, he must pay the penalty that would have been inflicted on the dependant (Exod. 20:16; Deut. 5:20; 19:16–21)

Lie and Truth

Lie is to deceive or lead astray by falsehood. It is strictly prohibited and mentioned in the scripture as a violation of trust. There are some Hebrew words for 'lie':

- *Remah*—to mislead (Ps. 10:7)
- *Saqar* (Exod. 20:16) —to tell a falsehood or deceive
- *Saw*—something as unreal (Deut. 5:20)
- *Kahash*—lack of dependability in a relationship
- *Patah*—enticing to do wrong

There are three Greek words in connection with 'lie':

1. *Planao*— 'to lead astray'
2. *Apatao*—to entice
3. *Doloo* or *dolioo*—to trick treacherously or trap another person[4]

The practice of lying destroys personal relationships. Lies are viewed negatively in the scripture. Satan is a liar and the father of lies. (John 8:42–47). God himself does not lie at all (Heb. 6:18). If we model our behaviour on God's pattern, we will surely rely on speaking the truth. God is the God of truth. A man of truth is a person whose words and deeds correspond. (Ps. 51:6). Truth is something in relation with reality and so it is reliable, accurate and trustworthy. False is unreliable because it distorts reality.

Telling the truth grimly and coldly to someone is like killing him. It is the lie that flatters smoothly and hides the truth. False praise and slander go hand in hand. Love without truth is lying and truth without love is deadly.

We live in a world where one must continually watch one's back. Trusting anyone is a risky affair. All humans have known, or will know, the disillusionment of believing in someone and then finding out that he or she had been lying all along. Every year millions of mates find out that their 'loving' husbands or wives had been cheating on them for a long period of time, while feigning faithfulness. Seemingly, trustworthy business people finally show their true colours after having cheated people of their life savings. Humans seem to look at lying as a mild transgression. It is an easy way to cover up inappropriate behavior while maintaining a semblance of integrity. The mind can easily rationalise lying.

Warning to Christians
Christians must be honest in their relationship with others. Scripture says, "Therefore each of you must put off falsehood and speak truthfully to his neighbour, for we are all members of one body" (Eph. 4:25). There is a very interesting insight into the way God thinks in Revelation 21:8—that all liars shall have their part in the lake of fire.

We have to test the words of our tongues in the light of the Word of God, because every evil word points to a corrupt heart, not yet regenerated. But every gentle word spoken reveals the spirit of Jesus in the heart. The Bible trains us in our daily life to highlight the good things and not to criticise others. We should think positively of our friends as well as our enemies, without lying. We should always strive to learn and tell the truth. Our lying tongues should be purified and we should receive new, spiritual tongues so that we may be able to pronounce the truth.

The Evil One deceived Eve and his cunning questions destroyed the truth, thereby placing God in doubt. In the same way, Satan approached Jesus to tempt Him. He did not respond with his own words; rather, replied, "It is written." Jesus affirmed the revealed word of God, which was in contrast to the tricks of the devil. There is no other way to overcome the father of lies than to depend on the word of God, which is the sword of the spirit.

Lying has poisoned our society. No one seems to be in favour of putting his or her trust in the other person. Lies isolate men and misunderstanding divides people. Truth is quickly subverted when people often slander others.[5]

We have to repent truly and always speak about people in their absence as if they were present. No white lies, no half-truths. We need to confess boldly our lies and subversive slander. We should not resort to half-truths or cover up with empty words and tricky explanations. We need the leading of the Holy Spirit so that we do not jeopardise the lives of other believers. We must always tell the truth.

Witness of Jesus

In relation to the mission of Jesus Christ, witness has a very specific meaning. John the Baptist was a witness to the truth (John 1:17; 5:33). He guided people to Lord Jesus, who came from God as a saviour. The ministry that Jesus performed is a witness, for it pointed to Jesus as Messiah. The Old Testament scriptures were another witness (John 5:36-39). Jesus came from God and revealed God to the world; He was a witness to the truth of God. His witness was supported by the witness of the father (John 3:11; 8:14-18).

Those who lived with Jesus were witnesses to the truth that he was the saviour of the world (1 John 1:1-3). Down through the centuries, Christians bear the same witness to him. The spirit bears witness within us. (John 15:26; 1 John 5:7). The disciples boldly bore witness to him as Lord and Messiah. They were personal eye-witnesses of the events related to Jesus. (Acts 2:22-24; 5:30-32; 13:27-31). Other Christians, in that period, also bore witness to Jesus Christ (Acts 20:24; 23:11). It is the solemn responsibility of the whole Church to be the effective witness of Lord Jesus Christ. Bearing witness to Jesus became so closely associated with being killed for Jesus' sake that the word for witness (Greek: *martyria*) produced the word 'martyr'[6] (Rev. 6:9; 17:6; 11:7; 12:11; 20:4). We should not give false testimony against anyone; rather, we should always be ready to bear witness of Lord Jesus Christ.

Conclusion

Humans would never make lying an offence of the highest magnitude. God did, because He knows the devastating societal and psychological consequences of deceit.[7] We have God to thank for this magnificent commandment, not man.

God knew the horrible consequences of lying. He knew that a society that condones lying would, in time, become an unlivable society, where the most cunning would rule.[8] Thus, in His love for humans, *and for the weak in particular*, He asserted that lying was an extremely serious sin, that it was unacceptable and that it would be punished severely.

Notes

1. W. E. Vine, An Expository Dictionary of the New Testament Words, p.120.
2. Don Fleming, Bible Knowledge Dictionary, p.461.
3. Fleming H. Revell, The Revell Bible Dictionary, p.370.
4. *Ibid.*, p.638.
5. Abd al-Masih, The Ten Commandments, p.183.
6. Don Fleming, Bible Knowledge Dictionary, p.461.
7. Fleming H. Revell, The Revell Bible Dictionary, p.646.
8. *Ibid.*, p.880.

No Coveting

You shall not covet your neighbour's house. You shall not covet your neighbour's wife or his manservant, his ox or donkey or anything that belongs to your neighbour (Exod. 20:17).

Introduction

Among the Ten Commandments, the last one forbids covetousness. This commandment deals with attitudes, whereas others deal with actions. Sins such as murder, adultery, stealing and lying are 'outward' sins, but covetousness is an 'inward' sin. A person may not be guilty of sinful action, but still be guilty of the hidden sin of covetousness (Matt. 5:21-30).

Sins start in the mind. Before adultery, stealing and some forms of killing, comes lust. Lust is an illicit and obsessive desire for what is not ours. Before adultery comes an obsessive lustful desire for another man's wife. Before stealing comes the desire for another man's property. To take another woman or to steal another person's property, some people are willing to kill.

Definition of Covetousness

Covetousness means to have an inordinate desire for (something belonging to another) or to be 'overly desirous of something.' It is to desire another person's possessions. The tenth commandment states that we are not to look longingly at someone's wealth or wife.

Covetousness has various shades of meaning, among which the most important are as follows:

- The desire to have something (1 Cor.12:31; 14:29).

- The inordinate desire to have something (Luke 12:15, Eph. 5:5. Col. 3:5).

- The excessive desire of what belongs to another[1] (Exod. 20:17; Rom. 7:7).

The sin of covetousness covers a wide range of unlawful and self-centred desires. Selfish ambitions, sexual lusts and common greed are all forms of covetousness (Deut. 5:21; 1 Tim. 6:9-10).

The prohibition against covetousness seems to look beyond the violent appropriation of another's property; it forbids that kind of thinking and willing (Prov. 6:25; Mic. 2:2). It is not confined to acquiring properties; it also bans enticing co-workers, servants or friends. It talks about attractive people and the things that we may desire. The Ten Commandments not only forbid our evil actions, but also condemn our hidden intentions.

Covetousness in the Old Testament

A great deal of the Old Testament law was intended to counteract the spirit of covetousness. The passionate desire for material possessions brings personal and spiritual disaster. It is so with every case of covetousness in scripture. Some of the outstanding examples of covetousness are: Achan (Josh. 7), Ahab (1 Kings 21) and Gehazi (2 Kings 20:27). A person is tempted to put a material object above God Himself, because covetousness involves focusing one's desire on that object.

It is the commandment against a negative way of thinking and willing. (Mic 2:2; Prov. 6:15). As the covetous person tries to get what he wants, his covetousness can produce all kinds of immoral and unlawful behaviour; such as stealing, oppression, deceit and violence (Exod. 20:17; Josh. 7:21). The practical application of this commandment is 'being satisfied with our own possessions and resources' (Deut. 5:21; 7:25; Prov. 28:16).

The New Testament on Covetousness

While the Old Testament puts our evil intentions and actions under the punishment of the law, the New Testament grants us deeper knowledge of our sinful nature and guides us to accept the righteousness of God through faith in Jesus Christ. The Law of Moses tries to prevent us from falling, but Jesus grants us victory over sin through complete justification and the power of the spirit of God. The grace of the triune God sets us free from our sin to His righteousness and leads us from defeat to victory by the power of His indwelling love.

Jesus presented the simple statement, "Deny yourself. Be content with what you have". But the commercials challenge,

'Desire everything. Buy whatever you do not have.' Jesus gave importance to spirituality, which leads us into eternity. (Matt. 16:26; Mark 8:35). He wants to restore us to Himself and enable us to look at all material things from His perspective. Spiritual truths are more valuable than material belongings.

Jesus warned that no one can serve two masters (God and money) at the same time. A choice must be ultimately made between them (Matt. 6:24). Jesus taught us liberty from things. We can be set free from such a terrible bondage. Furthermore, Jesus said, "Not so with you; instead whoever wants (desire) to become great among you must be your servant" (Matt. 20:26). The desire to become famous or great is unspiritual.

The apostles of Christ knew why it was important to be satisfied with what they had and be liberated from increasing debts, which can destroy the soul and the body. The epistle of James traces the origin of temptation. He affirms that temptation is not from God. If anyone is tempted, he is drawn away by the desire of his flesh and blood.

Paul cried out that his great desire was to know Christ. May it be ever the same with us. Paul's realisation of this in his own experience helped him to see the incurable sinfulness of human nature (Rom. 7:7-11; Mark 7:22-23). To him, covetousness is a form of idolatry. A person's selfish desires may be so strong that the thing he covets takes the place of God in his life.[2] (Col. 3:5). Paul calls a greedy individual an idolater. The thing he wants so badly becomes a god to him, for it determines the choices he will make (Eph. 5:5).

We are expected to care about other persons when using things. Often it is reversed, so that human beings care about things and use people. We should not be much careful about things; rather, we should be careful about the rights of other people. We have to share our material possessions with those in need, instead of coveting the possessions of someone else. Dan Betzer writes, "The history of this world has been stained and darkened by the crimes to which nations and individuals have been driven by the spirit of covetousness. This is spiritual corruption, the gangrene of the soul, and indulgence in unholy desires. Covetousness becomes a master."[3]

The tenth commandment forbids our evil actions and condemns our hidden intentions. To a certain extent, the court can judge the actual crimes of a person, but man's heart can be discerned only by God. We normally do not fully understand our stubborn and unclean hearts. It is a fact that no one is to avoid temptation, but everyone is called to resist evil with all his or her heart. We have to watch temptation from the very beginning, resist it and overcome it. Dr. Martin Luther said, "I cannot prevent the birds from flying over my head; but I can prevent them from nesting in my hair."[4]

How can we overcome this sin? The Bible says that we are to set our affections on things above, not on the things of the earth. Also, as we study the word of God, the Holy Spirit may cause us to have an insatiable appetite for spiritual truth and a desire to grow in grace day by day. Christian believers ought to allow God's word to discipline their desires, their goals and their intentions daily. Besides, overcoming unclean thoughts depends on our total surrender to Jesus and His eternal grace that we may pray confidently.[5] We should not sin deliberately, for the Holy Spirit sanctifies our thoughts and attitudes. Jesus wants us to be victorious in all our thoughts. Our thoughts must be completely cleansed by the blood of Jesus Christ. In addition, only sincere love for God and other people is helpful for us to have the right perspective in this context. The Christians can resist temptation for covetousness through exercising sacrificial love. They will then be devoted to God.

Conclusion

God, who created the human mind, knows its dynamics better than anyone else. He knows the steps to sin. Lust is step one before a multitude of sins (James 1:14-15). In His great wisdom, He concludes His commandments with a preventative command: "Stop the thought and you'll stop the action."

We are to place the highest value on people, not on their possessions. All persons are important to God. This commandment strikes beneath the surface of the covetous act, tracing evil conduct and evil desire and probing the hidden motives of men. It highlights the pivotal importance of wrong appetites and intentions. Like our parents, God gives us commandments to help keep us focused on what is most important and how to stay safe. All of His guidance is meant to keep us safe, help us stay close to Him and, in the end, to give us *more* freedom and happiness.

The word 'commandment' might make us consider the Ten Commandments as a list of 'Thou Shalt Nots.' God does not only tell us what we should not do; He also tells us what we 'should' do. His greatest hope is for our eternal happiness, so we can be sure that His commandments are not restrictive rules; they are divine guidance meant to protect us from harm and lead us to better ways of living.

A Final Word

The Ten Commandments are one of the greatest proofs of God's existence; they are a powerful expression of divine love for humanity. They were conceived by the Creator to prevent humans from following false gods; they are meant to prevent behaviours that eventually bring about havoc and turmoil in society. A close analysis of these commandments also reveals that they were meant to protect the weak, the powerless and the righteous from the abuse of those who have power and those who are callous and insensitive towards the rights of others.

The time has come to re-assert the divinity, nobility, dignity, holiness and great benefits of these God-enunciated commandments and to combat the arrogant and dangerous efforts of people who want society to stumble evermore towards degradation and self-destruction.

Notes

1. Merril. C. Tonney (Ed), The Zondervan Pictorial Bible Dictionary, p.187.
2. Don Fleming, Bible Knowledge Dictionary, p.79.
3. Dan Betzer, The Ten Commandments, p.28.
4. Abd al-Masih, The Ten Commandments, p.197.
5. *Ibid.*, p.198.

Bibliography

1. Alexander, Pat: *The Lion Encyclopedia of the Bible*, (A Lion book, Sydney 1987).
2. Al-Masih, Abd: *The Ten Commandments*, (Light of Life, Austria).
3. Betzer, Dan: *The Ten Commandments*, (AOG, Springfield, 1990).
4. Douglous, J. D.: *New Bible Dictionary*, (Intervarsity Press, London, 1982).
5. Fleming, Don: *Bible Knowledge Dictionary* (Pilot's Book Co., U.S.A. 1990).
6. Mathew Henry's Commentary, (Hendrickson Publishers, USA, 1993).
7. Rad, Gerhard Von: *Moses* (USCL, London, 1960).
8. Revell, Fleming H.: T*he Revell Bible Dictionary*, (Baker Book House Co., Michigan, 1994).
9. Tonney, Merril C.(Ed): *The Zondervan Pictorial Bible Dictionary*, (Zondervan Publishing House, Michigan, 1967).
10. Vine, W. E.: *An Expository Dictionary of New Testament Words* (Fleming H. Revell Co., New Jersey, 1966).

www.ingramcontent.com/pod-product-compliance
Lightning Source LLC
Chambersburg PA
CBHW032128090426
42743CB00007B/518